GAIN AN EDGE AT JOB INTERVIEWS

GAIN AN EDGE AT JOB INTERVIEWS

Jeff Tapper

LIBRARY OF CONGRESS CONTROL NUMBER:		2014912228
ISBN:	HARDCOVER	978-1-4990-1276-7
	SOFTCOVER	978-1-4990-1277-4
	EBOOK	978-1-4990-1280-4

Rev. date: 07/11/2014

To order additional copies of this book, contact:
Xlibris LLC
1-800-455-039
www.Xlibris.com.au
Orders@Xlibris.com.au
615699

CONTENTS

Section 1: Understanding Interviews

Section 2: Preparing for Interviews

Section 3: The Actual Interview

Section 4: Post-Interview Strategies

Section 5: Practice Questions

Preface

This book has been written with the goal of providing you with a complete guide to what can be done to increase chances of selection for the job for which you have applied. It has been written for a wide range of possibilities, and thus you can choose the parts relevant to your situation. It is also full of many practical tips to ponder and traps to avoid, which are general to all interviews.

Although your final selection for a job can never be guaranteed, you will significantly increase your chances through research, good preparation, and use of the many strategies outlined. This book will guide you through that process.

Strategies are included under the three main stages in the interview process:

1. preparation and research
2. being effective during the interview
3. affecting the outcome after the interview.

The initial section of this book will focus on interview types and any pre-interview screening. This will be followed by guidance on recommended actions under the preparation phase. We will then go through the stages from what to do on the day of the interview and also importantly after the interview.

The book includes a set of thirty-five commonly asked questions and guidance on effective answers. The latter portion of the book lists numerous other possible interview questions sorted by selection criteria and attributes from which you can choose the most relevant to your industry and desired post and then use them to practise.

People who conduct interviews may also find this book useful as a question bank resource as there are over 900 questions in the sample section alone.

Throughout this book, the use of words to describe the employer—such as 'business', 'organisation', or 'company'—can be used interchangeably. This is also true for the work unit, which could be a team, section, department, or division.

Section 1

Understanding Interviews

Introduction

Purpose of the Interview

Interviews serve many purposes including:

- to determine if you are the right person for the job
- to provide an opportunity to develop initial relationships
- to provide an opportunity to gain more information by either party
- to ensure that you fully understand the post to be filled, including any out-of-hours commitments
- to screen or test you against the required characteristics/skills/ attitudes or criteria for the work
- to clarify or verify claims made in writing, which for some jobs may include a skills test, such as typing
- to determine whether your personal qualities and attitudes will fit the current culture
- to determine if you are suitable to proceed to another stage in the selection process, such as a second interview
- to negotiate conditions of employment
- to determine how much supervision you may require
- to determine what you offer compared to others
- to basically get to know you in the shortest possible time.

The overall aim is to allow managers to determine your potential and predict future on-the-job performance against what is required and then rank all applicants to facilitate a decision on the final selection.

What the Employer Wants

The employer doesn't know you, and judging a person on a written application alone carries risks such as:

- misrepresentation of your abilities (fraudulent claims)
- interpersonal or communication issues not obvious from the written application
- potential understatement of your abilities
- insufficient information to judge your capabilities
- an inability to assess how you will behave (perform) under differing circumstances
- being unable to compare you to other applicants to make a selection.

A written application will not usually indicate whether you have all the required knowledge or skills and whether you will fit in with the culture at that workplace. Communication abilities are often very important in jobs, and that cannot be well assessed on only the written word. The interview also allows body language to aid in the communication process, which allows for more effective judgement of the truth of what you are saying at the interview and also to explore different aspects of your answers.

The employer is thus trying to fill in the gaps and also determine your personal attributes and whether you are likely to stay. They also have the opportunity to tell you more about the work and provide information on the benefits of working for them.

Why the Employer Takes Selection So Seriously

There must be some return for the time and expense incurred through advertising and the business time lost by the selection process. There will be reduced work output as the new workers must train for the work and build their in-house knowledge and skills. During this time, new workers also distract more skilled persons away from their jobs while they provide the required supervision. The selected person must also present the required image and manner to their customers, or else the business may have negative consequences to its reputation. They must have the current skills or potential to manage the work requirements whether they are technical or people-oriented.

If they choose the wrong person for the job, then they may be faced with performance problems, interpersonal conflicts, damaged business efficiency and effectiveness, work injuries, and increased wastage of their product. At times, the whole process may even have to be repeated if the person they selected must be sacked or quits as the work didn't meet their expectations. The latter point also implies that you should do proper research into the work before applying in order to reduce the possibility of a poor fit and job dissatisfaction.

Initial Stages of Selection

Don't Let the Paperwork Let You Down

Your written application may be considered and even scored against other applicants' paperwork to determine a shortlist for the interview. This is why attention to detail is essential. Selection criteria statements must be comprehensive and competitive. Consider some expert input at that stage.

Although beyond the scope of this book, it is important to make a few points about the original application. It is essential that the cover letter is addressed to the correct person with the correct spelling and that it clearly identifies the actual job applied for. The latter is important as the business or organisation may have many jobs advertised at any point in time, and they need to know which one you are seeking. If providing an email address as a means of contact, then please ensure it is appropriate and professional, even if this means setting up a new account separate to that for your friends.

If you have applied for multiple jobs using the same letter, ensure you have made appropriate changes and tailored your response to what the business is seeking. The latter information may be sourced from the job advert, any selection criteria, or other research into the company.

Writing a first-class application letter is vital to getting selected for interview, particularly in a competitive market. The length of the application is usually guided by the employer, who may supply a form to complete or suggest a limit on the total number of pages that you can submit. This is often only a few pages so that the employer can review each curriculum vitae (CV) quickly for shortlisting. If a limitation does not apply, still keep your application papers concise, and include all relevant details that relate to what they are looking for. Generally, the cover letter is brief, and most details are included in the attached CV.

Check for typing and grammatical errors. Word processors have a spelling-and-grammar checker. Use it, and then proofread it also as the wrong word may be accepted by the spellchecker! Avoid submitting written work that has errors obviously corrected or crossed out.

Use good paper, not paper that is crumpled, torn out of a pad, includes inappropriate fancy patterns, etc. Employers usually prefer typed paperwork though they may ask for a handwritten application. Check if you are unsure of the required standard. Those who prefer handwritten ones are looking for neatness as an indicator of taking pride and care in your work. Some handwriting is usually necessary with respect to completing standard 'application for employment' forms. Take care when completing these. Ensure that you read any instructions and questions prior to commencement on the form. Errors and messily completed forms may again rule you out at this stage. Consider practising on a photocopy first. Apply caution when completing the name section as they may require either the first name or the surname to be placed first, and these may appear in different boxes. Ensure that you follow any requested order of required responses (e.g. work history from the latest to the oldest work or vice versa).

Format your work into paragraphs with headings and not just a block of text.

If the employer requests a photo of you, then ensure you are dressed as if for an interview. Do not provide a photo if it is not requested as it will not always work in your favour. It can allow bias based on how you look before you even reach the next stage.

Ensure your application is delivered as soon as possible if no closing date is given. If there is a closing date, then ensure it reaches the employer before the close. Consider using registered mail for added security and priority for this mail. If submitting via email, then ensure it is sent earlier than the closing date to allow for possible network outages. Dropping off an application in person may also be possible, but get a written acknowledgement from an employee that it has been received by the employer.

Make a Pre-Interview Positioning Call

To gain a further edge in being selected for the work, try contacting the key decision-maker prior to the interview. Their names may have been in the job advert, or you may need to call to discover who will be interviewing you. There is usually a name for enquiries; otherwise, try the Human Resources (Personnel) Department or the actual department that is responsible for the position. By being in contact prior to an interview, you are already establishing a relationship which will potentially make both you and the interviewer more comfortable on meeting at the interview.

Tip: Be cautious as some adverts will state that you must not contact the business in this way but await an invitation for an interview. To go counter to their request may lead to your rejection.

Confirm if your résumé has been received and ask if there is a specific time frame for the job to be filled. Note that online applications may provide a receipt number. Find out if it is a new job, a replacement, or a temporary one; and if it is the last, then what are the chances of its continuing? In some organisations, for various reasons, temporary posts may be common and may present ongoing opportunities. In that circumstance, they can almost guarantee ongoing work opportunities. This information can be helpful to know. If it is a new post, then the employer will be more receptive to any innovative ideas you may give about the work. If it is a replacement situation, then the employer will probably use the last person as a benchmark and thus compare you to them. If the last person was dismissed due to poor performance, then there will likely be a higher sensitivity to skill deficiencies, and you will thus need to build confidence in your potential very quickly.

Note that, in some selection processes, there are other preliminary stages as follows.

Preliminary or Screening Interviews

Screening interviews (sometimes described as first-round interviews) are usually short and are designed as a quick test focused on a few questions related to those job-selection criteria that are considered the most critical to successful selection.

Screening interviews are predominantly used when there are a large number of suitable applicants to be shortlisted. Selecting staff from only the written applications runs the risk of missing some suitable candidates whose talents may have been understated or wasting time on those who may have overstated their claims. At times, an external employment agency may be utilised to conduct this process. They will provide the shortlist to the employer. When conducted by the employer, the method may vary from brief formal interviews to informal social-type gatherings. In the latter, you may be assessed by several people while circulating at what appears as a social gathering. This will demonstrate how you present yourself, along with being able to assess your social and communication skills. Take care to treat these interviews with as much care as the main interview and to accord any agency staff the same respect as the employer.

Sometimes a full interview may have been used, but the selectors have trouble choosing the final candidate. They then may shortlist on the first round and then re-interview the most promising candidates. At times, more than two rounds may be needed. This is especially so for executive appointments.

Assessment Centres

Assessment centres for bulk hiring of staff can be used in either public or private sectors and involve mass testing of candidates for jobs. However, an initial screening process may have already occurred prior to this stage. It can be at any location chosen by the employer or those subcontracting to do the testing. In other words, it may not be a recognised centre but is more descriptive of the process to be used. They may utilise tests, group or individual meetings, team exercises, case studies, performances, or interviews over more than one day. Ask the contact person arranging the session on what to expect. This process is usually used to source entry-level staff, such as for new graduates or training schemes. They may also be useful for selecting staff in call centres, sales, low-level admin, etc.

Assessments can be designed to be relevant to the work in question, but others are standardised across the industry. Not all jobs or work tasks are amenable to testing in this way. If appropriate, it may include actual work tasks, such as typing letters or other clerical duties. There may be a written test on how you meet their job criteria. Other activities may include presenting to a group (e.g. PR roles or performing arts), role-playing situations (e.g. in sales, 'Sell me this widget'), mock meetings, and even leadership or creativity problem-solving exercises. The last exercises aim to see how you perform in a group, what role you adopt, etc. The activity may involve solving a puzzle as a team or building something from supplied parts, such as paper and adhesive tape. This is more about the process and roles people adopt than how good-looking the result may be!

Strategically, they are observing you for teamwork, mediation where necessary, not being argumentative, being focused on the task, plus participation and potential leadership (when necessary to the role). Some group exercises may induce competitiveness and conflict, so remain flexible, appropriately assertive when needed, and calm.

An example of mass screening is when people are selected for performing arts, such as TV idol-type series or reality shows.

Another common test in management, administrative, or clerical jobs may include sorting out an in tray and explaining your priorities and actions. This may be made more realistic through adding unread emails and voicemails. In deciding your priorities, consider the issue from the perspective of importance-versus-urgency dimensions. If a task is both urgent and important, it takes priority. On the other hand, if it is not urgent or important, then it has the lowest priority. Also consider business goals and possible delegation when deciding priorities. Spell out your strategies and actions, such as file the item, read the item, delegate it, or act on it.

Case studies may be conducted individually or in a group. They will involve a business situation which includes the background information and involves determining strategies for a successful outcome. There may be ambiguous or extraneous information to sort through and may include a time limit to give some pressure to the exercise.

Tip: ensure you are prepared to state any assumptions made or reasons for making your action recommendation.

The best preparation for these tests is to re-examine the job duties and then consider which skills may be tested. Consider what problem scenarios you may face at work as these will most likely form part of the test.

Examples may include:

- managing somebody being disruptive at a meeting
- managing a difficult customer
- being able to deliver a difficult staff appraisal
- managing conflict at work
- managing the consequences of staff being on sick leave
- facilitating good teamwork with a new group of people
- being able to correctly shelve inventory by code numbers.

Be on your best behaviour as often management or supervisory staff may also be participating, even if it is in meeting candidates over tea or lunch breaks. The others being assessed may also become future work colleagues.

Recruitment Agencies

Recruitment agencies are in place to provide a service to an employer who does not have time to conduct initial interviewing and handle enquiries so they outsource this function to the agency. This is common in non-technical positions, such as administration, labour, and other positions where there is likely to be multiple candidates. The agency will conduct interviews with the view of providing the employer with a small shortlist of two or three of which they may then choose one or two to interview. It is important to treat the agency interview in the same way you would treat any other interview.

The other service a recruitment agency can provide is to fill hard-to-find positions. Usually, the employer has already advertised or tried to find a staff member through other means, and this has been unsuccessful. They then turn to a recruitment agency to broaden the search and provide them with more candidates to consider—e.g. qualified medical professionals (dentists, GPs), tax accountants, car mechanics. Occupational shortages will vary over time and in different locations.

Depending on contracts between the agency and the other business, the agency may not get paid their fee until the suggested person has stayed a defined period. This is to ensure they provided an acceptable employee who, in fact, stays and thus proves worthy of the cost. The employer is thus less likely to suffer rorting by the agency. Reputable agencies will accept this arrangement as being fair as they must maintain a good industry reputation. At other times, they may employ staff as contractors and assign them to the business, and thus the agency remains the employer and will charge the other business an hourly fee.

They may also be utilised to source staff for urgent or unique requirements—e.g. new business start-ups, business relocations involving significant physical inventory movement with a quick turnaround, or special-event staffing. They may also seek and provide short-term temp staff for leave cover or vacant shifts—e.g. nursing shifts, administrative temps.

In some industries, they are the preferred source to find staff, and thus you are wise to approach the agency for an interview. The agencies can be used as a surrogate Human Resources Section to help the business save on their own employment costs.

Agencies are contacted frequently by jobseekers, and they thus create a database of potential job candidates. There is a growing number of people listing their CVs on websites in order to find new employment, and thus agencies sometimes source staff from this media also. Note that agencies and employers may check social media profiles for information on personality, character, interests, professionalism that likely fit into the employer's culture. This may be especially true for graduates who have little work experience to highlight and are thus relatively unproven at work.

If you are on an agency's database of candidates, the agency will sometimes alert prospective employers to suitable applicants on their lists. In this case, they usually apply confidentiality rules to maintain your anonymity and instead utilise a reference number. If the employer is interested in you, the agency will provide more information to determine the suitability for an interview.

It is recommended that you request the agency to inform you prior to submitting your CV to any particular employer. In this way, you can prevent wasting time by deciding if that is actually a place you would want to work in or not. Ensure that you clarify the process they will follow in seeking your employment and who will be your ongoing contact person at the agency.

The service by the agency generally costs nothing to the person seeking employment as they recoup their costs from the eventual employer. There are some agencies that are subsidised by the government and thus charge no fees to the employer. Another benefit sometimes offered by agencies is career advice or critique on your CV.

Therefore, when meeting with agency staff for an interview, it is wise to ascertain if it is for an actual vacant position or for judging your value to add to their database for future opportunities. The latter situation may not be suitable if you are in a hurry to find work but can be an advantage if you are in no hurry. Agencies screen applicants for suitability and will quickly reject those that don't appear to be quality candidates as their reputation is on the line with their clients.

They are seeking enthusiastic and motivated people who may have some flexibility in choosing from a range of job opportunities. You can negotiate what salary and conditions of employment you are seeking, and they can then negotiate on your behalf with prospective employers.

In Australia, respectable agencies are licensed employment agents and are a member of the governing body, which is the Recruitment and Consulting Services Association (RCSA). If you have a complaint about an agency, you can lodge it with the RCSA. Note that if you use an unlicensed agency, it is at your own risk. If you are from another country, please check your local regulations on how reputable agencies are recognised.

Tip: treat your interview at an agency as you would treat any other job interview, and dress the part.

Headhunters

An unexpected call may be received, inviting your interest in applying for a job or attending a preliminary interview. This is usually referred to as headhunting, and their list of candidates may be identified through industry intelligence or by the prospective employer. They may also troll social media sites, such as LinkedIn or Facebook, for candidates. In addition, they may check résumés on online databases. Headhunting often applies to senior management, professional occupations, executive-level positions, or a job requiring unusual requirements.

Good headhunters will already know you through their research—you will be surprised how much they know about you and your career! They will have you already pre-qualified as being suitable for the position they seek to fill. In many cases, the client has suggested your company as a place they would like to target staff from. This is especially true when you currently work for a company that is considered a leader in their field.

The headhunters will ask to meet you for coffee or will ask permission to phone you after hours. They will usually let you know immediately who their client is, all the salary and career conditions, etc. to avoid wasting time if you are not a good match. To increase your chances of being headhunted, make sure you have a current online profile (e.g. LinkedIn) that includes your mobile number!

A high degree of discretion is usually applied in this process as certainly animosity can be generated if a business is seen as poaching staff from another business. Thus, they may at times only disclose the potential employer at a later stage in the process. You are thus at some disadvantage in not knowing full information about the job, and they are evaluating your suitability without you knowing the selection criteria!

Tip: As you cannot do your general research into a job with an unknown employer, it is recommended that you enquire about the skills and experience being sought. You can then prepare accordingly.

As you were approached about changing work, you need to consider your desire to change now and what additional benefits you can negotiate to make it worth your while.

Types of Interviews: What to Expect

Basic Structures

A general categorisation of interview structures includes the following:

Informal—This interview has no particular structure and could be described as freewheeling, where the interviewer will allow the interview to be guided according to responses made. Hence, there are no set series of questions, and each applicant may have entirely different interviews, making it less objective. However, it can give the astute interviewee (you) a chance to direct the conversation towards areas of strength. The interviewer has the freedom to take the interview in directions to judge what kind of person you are and how you will react in different situations and to primarily determine if you fit in with the relevant team or perhaps organisational culture.

Structured—The interviewer will usually tell you what is to happen near the beginning. Listen! A series of set questions will usually be used for all applicants so that the interview is fairer and thus all will have the same chance of succeeding. This allows responses to be scored. This method is often used in the public sector, where equity laws prevail. The interviewer will usually not paraphrase the question but can repeat the question if you asked. This is not to say that probing questions may not be asked if they want greater clarity on your answer.

Semi-structured—It is a mixture of both structures previously mentioned. There will appear to be a mix of set questions and open discussion, with the interviewee allowed to travel to different subject areas if it keeps the interviewer's interest.

All Interviews Are Not the Same: Interview Methods

The above structures may apply to any of the types that follow:

Coming In for a Chat or Informational Interviews

Being invited to come and meet with the employer or their representative, possibly over a coffee, may seem friendly and casual. However, all meetings with potential employers should be treated with care, and they call for your best behaviour even if supposedly only for an informal chat. Job offers may eventuate.

Tip: You can use this event to have some of your questions answered about working for the industry or a particular company, including the career opportunities or organisational structure. Use this time wisely to build your relationship.

Computer Interviews

As with the screening interview, this may be a tool used to ask questions and compare applicants, especially with larger numbers of applicants. It may be an automated session or may be interactive with the screener.

Courtesy Interviews

You may get an informal interview, although probing questions may still be used. This may not be for an actual vacancy, but it is an opportunity to evaluate you for possible future posts and establish a relationship with the employer. This can help later, especially for temporary posts, when the usual formalities may be waived to get a quick starter. By becoming employed on a temporary contract, you will gain inside information on future permanent jobs and what the employer is looking for.

Job Fairs/Expos

Attending a job fair or expo can provide access to information on many potential employers. They are usually advertised in your local paper, TV, or email bulletins and may include both exhibitors and relevant presentations.

Tip: Be prepared for an on-the-spot interview when at a booth and thus also dress appropriately. You will read later how first impressions do count!

Have several copies of your résumé on hand. Take business or contact cards if you have them, plus a pen and notepad to take notes. Take the opportunity to find out what you can about their business as useful preparation for a future formal interview.

Meal Interviews

Another variation usually reserved for higher-level, private-sector posts is where you are invited out to meet with the contact person or employer over a meal. The interviewer may have chosen this method as they are too busy to meet in their usual work time. It can also indicate that you are a very desirable candidate, so start considering your desired conditions of employment. Ensure you know in advance how to find the venue and where to park if using your own vehicle.

Tip: Be prepared for a quick assessment and not necessarily a long lunch. Be on guard with your behaviour, just as in more-formal interviews.

Assuming that you are also invited to eat, be decisive in what you order. Consider avoiding the most expensive dishes as their good and generous nature may only go so far! It is suggested that it is from the middle of the range in costs rather than high-cost items, and take care if drinking alcohol (better to avoid). Remember, alcohol may cause you to let down your guard and at the least may cause muddled thinking.

Avoid very messy food choices as it may not be a good look with food spilt in your lap or across your shirt! Use manners at the table, including not talking with your mouth full. Try not to push too many special requests or variations to the menu option as you may look too fussy and maybe high-maintenance! Try to match the interviewer in the sense that if they do not take entrée or dessert, then don't either.

Tip: don't pick up the bill at the end of the meeting, and do thank the host on departure.

Panel Interviews

In this process, a group of interviewers will be present and may take turns in asking questions, or there may be a chairperson who will direct all or majority of the questions. At times, certain persons may attend as observers of the process, such as Human Resources personnel to ensure procedures are adhered to or other staff who may be attending to learn the process. This is the method most commonly used by the public (government) sector (including education, teaching, and police amongst others) and may also be used to select high-level posts in private businesses. The decision is made at the end after all candidates have been interviewed.

Panel members usually take turns to ask questions that reflect the area of their special interest or experience. The chairperson will usually open and close the interview process.

Panel interviews are considered to be fair as there is less chance of personal bias affecting the outcome. Members often score or vote on the selected candidate(s). A gender mix is also commonly used in the public sector to hedge against gender bias in selection. A panel will often have an odd number of members to avoid a deadlock in voting, thus allowing for a majority decision if the results are tight.

Tip: Accept business cards if they are offered, and have them on the desk in front of you as it may help remember names. It is good to use the panel members' names when able as people like to hear their own names.

Presentations

The selection process may include a presentation on a given topic, especially for higher-level posts. It may be delivered to either a small or large group or even fellow candidates at an assessment centre. The topic may be given in advance so that it can be prepared prior to the interview. They may provide background information to analyse or only a topic on which to speak. In other commercial positions, there may even be a marketing plan to prepare.

Apply good presentation skills, including eye contact with the audience, speaking clearly and confidently at the correct pace with the appropriate audiovisual aids, and timing. Pay attention to both a clear introduction and final summary in your presentation. Research optimal use of tools like PowerPoint for elements such as colours, font size, lines per page, themes, autotiming, inserted graphics.

Tip: Remember to practise your timing and delivery, utilising any tools you will need on the day, such as PowerPoint. Also ensure that any saved electronic presentations are in a compatible version with their software.

Registration Interviews

This is usually associated with recruitment companies that will evaluate you for a range of possible future posts. Generally, this is for temporary positions, but they may also market you to companies for a finder's fee on permanent work. It is thus advisable to know whether you are attending a real job interview or they are assessing you for future posts.

Screening Interviews

This is the first-level process to screen out unsatisfactory applicants, especially if there is a large number of applicants. It may be conducted by a third party, such as a recruitment agency, or an HR consultant. It is an initial fact-finding mission to clarify your background experience, knowledge, skills, and attitudes. The process may evaluate a limited number of key selection criteria. In other words, do you meet the job specifications, and do you perhaps present yourself as well as your CV may suggest?

Single-Person Informal Interviews

Meeting one-to-one with a manager or their representative is often favoured by smaller organisations or businesses but is thus subject to personal biases. However, that can work both ways, so it is a chance to impress on your personal appearance and friendly, likable attitude.

Situational Assessments

You may actually be placed in an artificial worksite and be given situations to perform under supervision. This is to judge how you may react in an actual worksite while experiencing a possibly challenging scenario. You will probably be watched by a group of people. A presentation or demonstration may also be requested.

Sequential Interviews

A series of interviews may be carried out by different interviewers in turn, where each makes their own opinion or assessment of the candidate's suitability and competitiveness. However, they may compare notes and provide follow-up questions in areas that you have already covered. Then they may meet as a group to compare notes and to decide on who to select or who to interview further. This process is often used by larger companies, but the final decision may be made by the most senior person participating.

Stress Interviews

In these interviews, you are deliberately put under pressure to see how you cope. This may be done through aggressive body language, use of voice, being uncomplimentary, using challenging questions, etc. This may be an applicable method for high-pressure jobs dealing with aggressive or potentially intimidating persons. You will still be asked similar questions to other interviews but maybe in a more challenging way, so preparation is still the key.

Tip: the way to deal with these is to remain calm and be polite in your responses, and don't take any of the comments personally.

The interviewer may start out with easy openers and then suddenly revert to a challenging question to catch you off guard. Multiple panel members may start to ask questions in rapid succession, thus placing you under increasing pressure.

Tip: Remember to keep calm, and if they allow insufficient time for you to answer, just stop and take charge of the situation. Compliment them on the questions they are asking, but say that if they want a complete answer, they will have to allow more time or to choose priority questions they want answered.

The priority at this point is to show confidence and calm, and not to sink under pressure. Recognising these tactics will help you deal with the situation more confidently in the future.

Telephone Interviews

This method may be used as it is considered to be quick, easy, and less costly than meeting in person. It may be used to verify background details to determine that the applicant is suitable to progress to the next stage. A full interview may also be conducted this way but usually only if you cannot be there in person (e.g. away on vacation). Telephone interviews are harder in the sense that it impedes normal communication as you are missing the essential element of body language, which is considered to account for 50 per cent of a conversation. Listening skills are thus also quite vital.

Tip: Indicate to the interviewer that you are both interested and listening by making the appropriate responses (e.g. 'Hmm', 'Yes', 'I see'). Project a friendly image by smiling often as you talk as it usually changes the voice in a way that projects such an image.

Use a positive voice, and convey enthusiasm for the work. Avoid mumbling into the phone, and follow the general-interview advice found elsewhere in this book. Make sure you are in a quiet place free of distractions and not eating or chewing at the time.

Don't forget that you can use notes and other paperwork while on the phone, so keep them on hand. It is best to prepare a summary or dot points for quick reference as you should not spend too much time looking for something in copious notes.

Use a phone that is reliable and not prone to dropouts. Don't stop to take another call while in an interview!

Tip: If you receive a surprise call, it may be better to ask if they can call you back after a short while, or better still, ask if they can hold a minute. This is to calm and gather your thoughts. You may ask if they wouldn't mind waiting a moment while you do something (e.g. close the door,

turn off the TV). This can give you time to get your notes ready to refer to and to calm your nerves.

Keep a diary or calendar on hand near the phone in case you need to book an in-person interview time. If you use a mobile (cell) phone for your diary, then you still may find it easier to have a paper diary ready while you talk.

Tip: If others live in the house with you, ensure they are aware that you may receive an interview call, and request that they handle the call appropriately! Also, request that they keep the noise down as it is amazing what background noise a phone can pick up.

Take notes on what insights you gain as you may be offered a second interview and you can learn from this first one. Request a face-to-face interview if you think the interview is going well. Use that second opportunity to clarify strengths and correct any bad impressions you may have created at the first interview.

Overall, your main goal must be to sell yourself well so that you get the opportunity to move to the next stage in the selection process.

Videoconferencing or Skype Interviews

This form of an interview is most likely a screening process and may create the first step towards an in-person interview later.

Treat these as you would with any other interview and still dress up for the occasion. Apply the same body language as you would in person.

If you are a beginner with videoconferencing, then ensure you practise to get the lighting right so your face can be seen and that you are positioned correctly in the video frame. If using a tablet computer or mobile phone, then keep it steady or on a stand to avoid blurred images.

Tip: watch out that you have nothing inappropriate in the view behind you!

Types of Interview Questions

Questions to Explain Your Actions

Behavioural, Scenario, or Situational Questions

This method may be employed to yield information concerning behaviour, analytic thinking, and decision-making. Examples of past behaviours may be sought, or a background situation will be provided and the interviewer will want to know what steps you would take in that situation.

This is sometimes referred to as behaviour description interviewing, and the theory behind this is that the best predictor of future behaviour or performance is past behaviour or performance in similar circumstances. This is especially true if the past behaviour is a recent example and also if a long-standing pattern is established. Questions may commence with 'Give me a specific example of when . . .'. Questions may appear to focus on negative situations, such as when things go wrong, and identifying what actions you took.

A framework on which to answer may be assisted by the acronym SAO, which stands for outlining the *situation*, then the *action* you took, and finally the *outcome*. Another common framework in use is the STAR method. This stands for the *situation*, *task* you had to perform to address the situation, the *actions* you took (what and how), and the *results*.

Should you be asked to describe a situation for which you have had no experience, tell the panel, and ask whether they would like you to answer from a theoretical perspective. Alternatively, offer to discuss something similar that you experienced. Behavioural questions relating to what you may do in theory should be answered by commencing with 'I would . . .', 'I will . . .', etc.

Tip: Always consider some examples prior to the interview, and as with weaknesses, try to choose examples with a positive learning outcome. The result should have led to a change in behaviour so that you can claim to handle such situations better now.

Hypothetical Questions

These questions may be less detailed than scenario questions and ask how you would deal with such a situation—e.g. 'What would you do if . . . ?' These questions are more predictable and can be dealt with in a hypothetical way. Thus, the interviewer may want to talk of real situations experienced such as in behavioural interviews. However, they may actually be testing your knowledge of the correct process and procedures—e.g. 'How would you deal with team conflict?'

Criterion Questions

This is where all the questions are associated with the particular requirements of the job, usually listed as selection criteria in the job description form (JDF), job specification form (JSF), or other similar document. The employer will often want you to address a particular criterion and provide a relevant example from your past. This is similar to the previously described competency-based questions but may initially be at a more general level—e.g. 'Consider how you have demonstrated your ability to communicate effectively versus your ability to write reports.'

Questions Designed to Lead or Trap You

Leading Questions

These questions seem to indicate a particular answer is needed—e.g. 'Don't you think you should have checked on the appointment time?' These are often used to make a point or lead you to a conclusion. Be aware that the point of view expressed may not represent the views of the interviewer.

Tip: Take care not to be defensive, but be prepared to state your reasons for acting in a certain way. It could be to catch you on issues of values or attitudes that the employer does not want in their employees.

Loaded Questions

Questions that may appear innocent may reveal more about you and the way you think than you realise. The advice given above in the leading-questions section also applies here. Some questions go beyond a statement type of answer and need the reasoning behind your answer—e.g. 'Everybody takes [read as 'steals'] something from work from time to time. What do you think about that?'

Tip: Obviously, they are checking your honesty by trying to trap you into agreeing that it is OK to steal no matter how small or inexpensive an object taken! It is never OK!

Other questions may concern timekeeping at work, sickies, bending the rules, or issues that relate to discrimination towards others. Refer to a later chapter on ways in which people may discriminate.

Stress Questions

The interviewer may try to invoke stress to see how you respond.

Tip: Remember to keep calm at interviews and to recognise such questions for what they are. Do not become defensive as that may be a negative emotional response they are trying to elicit!

Other Common Question Types

Broad-Brush Questions

These may be used to open a discussion and gather initial information—e.g. 'Tell me about your last job'. Although this may seem a little laid-back in style, your communication style and ability to convey information in an organised and logical fashion is under test. These questions do not easily show what the interviewer is looking for.

Tip: Be careful not to delve into negative experiences or situations if you can avoid it. You don't want to leave the impression that trouble follows you or that you may present the same problems at the new job!

Clarification Questions

Usually, a straightforward question may be designed to clarify a point that is not easily ascertained from the written application. It may also be to clarify a view on something or be about your willingness to do certain aspects of the work (e.g. overtime, shift work, or start date).

Tip: Don't apply for jobs if you are not willing to work the hours required. Try to have researched the requirements fully prior to the interview.

Closed Questions

These questions are used when a definite yes/no type of answer is needed—e.g. 'Have you supervised staff before?'

Tip: It is best to not just reply with yes or no at times, but this doesn't mean you can ramble or take up too much time as a quick answer is needed. Try to mention skills, experience, or knowledge that have prepared you fully for the job at hand, but keep it brief. You must take every opportunity to sell yourself and prove you are the one to choose!

Competency-Based Questions

Questions may directly relate to the job skills, knowledge, attitudes, and how you approach the task or situation. You may also need evidence from past employers or from skills-based training to prove your competency. Often in industry, particular 'tickets' are required as an essential qualification (e.g. forklift ticket).

Educational-Background Questions

You may be asked information on your academic subjects and performance in your education years. Generally, this is more relevant to candidates in their early career, school-leavers, etc. This can also be applicable to positions with higher academic requirements. You may also be asked about any organising committees or other activities that may show dedication and involvement.

Fact Questions

These are enquiries about work experiences, educational background, or events to better explain the situation to the interviewers. The question may be aimed at bringing out the facts to judge the relevance of a claim being made by the applicant in writing or in person at the interview. This is similar to clarification questions previously described.

Multiple-Part Questions

These questions may include different parts or subquestions. They are difficult and rely on good listening and memory skills. Alternatively, you may be given a question to read, particularly if it involves analysing some information before answering—e.g. 'Teamwork is essential in this business. Can you tell us why you think it's important, what makes you a team player, and what you do to enhance collaboration?'

Tip: if you have trouble remembering, consider either writing down the parts of the question or asking that the question be repeated.

Open-Ended Questions

These are questions that cannot be answered with a simple yes or no. They encourage discussion—e.g. 'Why do you want to work here?'
The interviewer may also be examining whether you can give an organised or structured answer—e.g. 'I would like to work here because (1) I have . . . (2) I offer . . . (3) my goal is to . . .'.

Tip: take care not to ramble and keep aware of time in structured interviews.

Probing Questions (Sometimes Referred to as Funnel Questions)

These questions are designed to narrow down the focus of the answer to areas of particular interest. After an open question, the interviewer may like to investigate something that was said, but in a more thorough manner. They will probe to find out more—e.g. 'Tell me more about . . .' or 'Can you explain why you . . . ?' They may use the old 'how, what, why, and when' approach to probe into all facets of the problem.

Tip: stay focused when answering and be mentally prepared for this kind of question to avoid feeling pressured.

Self-Appraisal (Reflection) Questions

These questions are designed to see if you can reflect on and appraise your own performance. The ability to learn by reflective practice can indicate a person who needs less direction, is more committed to what they do, and can learn more easily from what they do. It may also be used to obtain honest answers that may be revealing—e.g. 'What abilities helped you do so well in your last job?' or 'What aspects of your last job presented difficulties?'

Tip: refer to other examples in the practice question lists at the end of this book.

Summary Question

This may involve paraphrasing or summarising one of your answers to confirm that you have been heard correctly—e.g. 'So what you said was . . . Is that correct?' This type of question may be used to confirm that you have said something negative, and they want to make sure they heard correctly before marking you down on it!

Tip: This may be a clue to reflect very quickly on what you said and make amends! It may also be a summary of positive points about your experience or abilities, so ensure all your points were included or be prepared to add additional points.

Technical Questions

For technical jobs, there may be questions on describing how you manage problems or carry out processes pertaining to the required work tasks. You should be able to draw on your experience.

Tip: be aware that you should probably mention any safety protocols you would observe as work accidents are very costly to all concerned.

Pre- or Post-Interview Testing

Purpose of Testing

Public and private sectors now frequently employ some form of testing in the screening and selection process. This would usually be prior to the interview but could be completed after the interview. Testing may include practical tests of ability, skill, and aptitude or may be focused on character or psychology.

Tip: if you have a disability that will make completion of the test difficult for you, let the employer know so that alternative formats may be considered.

Employers favour tests because they are relatively cheap, quick, objective (and thus fairer) in their potential to identify the best person for their job requirements. However, tests may prove less reliable when testing those with poor English or from different ethnic and cultural groups than those from the local population. According to M. Parkinson (*Interviews Made Easy: How to Get the Psychological Advantage*, Kogan Page, 1995), tests are claimed to increase an employer's ability to choose the right person by as much as 25 per cent. They are thus considered to provide more-reliable selection results than the interview alone. Remember that interviewers are subject to many personal biases, and testing helps overcome that shortcoming.

Ability and personality tests are the commonest tests used, especially as ability tests are considered good predictors of future performance.

Consider that tests can reinforce your claim to do the work, not just to highlight any weaknesses. They are designed to test how you match the employer's wish list. If you prove to be a poor fit, then they have saved you some lost time and grief embarking on a job that will not work out.

Tip: As a motivational thought, consider that your chances of getting the job are much improved by simply attending the test. This is because a number of applicants are too scared to turn up for the test!

Types of Tests

Group Discussion Method

At times, an employer may want to have candidates demonstrate their abilities, such as leadership, thinking on their feet, communication skills, or analytic skills, by taking part in a group discussion. It may also take the format of a debate on a current topic or be a problem-solving scenario.

Handwriting Tests/Analysis

Some employers may request a sample of your handwriting. They may be subjecting this to handwriting analysis (graphology). It is believed that handwriting can reveal much about a person.

Tip: You can compare your own writing with examples in analysis books found either in bookstores, maybe the local library, or via online search results. Consider whether a change is necessary to create a better impression.

IQ Tests

An IQ test can test your general intelligence and ability to think quickly. This is a written test where you have to answer a series of questions in a given time. Your results are compared to the 'average' person, and a category is assigned, such as 'above average'.

Tip: if you expect to perform an IQ test, then purchase and practise with a sample question book.

Leadership and Problem-Solving

You may be asked to work in a group-based, problem-solving exercise while also competing against other groups. The tasks are designed to assess problem-solving, teamwork, natural leadership skills, working under pressure, creativity, etc. They may involve building an item with limited resources and instructions—e.g. a bridge must be made from newspaper and adhesive tape, which must then hold a set weight for a designated time without collapsing.

Another example with the same resources may be to build the tallest tower that stays upright.

Personality Tests

Employers are putting more focus on soft skills, such as relationship building, collaboration, positive attitude, self-confidence, and communication skills. It is believed that these skills or attributes may provide a further competitive edge for the business or can engender a more harmonious workplace. An employee who has both the technical skills for the job and the soft skills would be ideal.

Standardised-questionnaire tests are done to show your personality type, values, and attributes. This may indicate whether you are introverted or extroverted, whether you are a conformist or nonconformist or assess other dimensions which have been found to account for observed behaviour. They may also show your attitudes, how you handle problems, and how you relate to others. In other words, they produce a personal profile.

The answers being sought will depend upon the job demands and also the desired personality that is required by the work team. The test may be done to confirm either a good or bad opinion about you as a candidate. The results may indicate to the interviewer where to use probing questions at the interview process. It can show how you may act when under pressure. Tests may range from an online version to a full three-hour assessment in a centre.

For some positions, especially those dealing with customers and supervising others, there may be interest in emotional intelligence (EI). Refer to D. Goleman, *Emotional Intelligence,* Bantam Books, 1995. It is asserted that higher levels of EI translate to better interpersonal skills and teamwork. Low EI means a low self-awareness and self-control of negative thoughts and emotions, which can adversely influence others in the workplace (e.g. attributes such as easy to upset, quick to anger). The factors associated with EI include:

- knowing your own emotions
- managing your emotions
- motivating yourself
- recognising emotions in others
- handling relationships.

Questions at an interview will be around testing your responses to these factors.

Tip: if you are able to get the results later, they can guide you on what needs attention for your own personal development.

Personality tests may be either a projective type or an objective type. The former is designed to have you fill in the blanks or describe something (e.g. the popular ink-blot interpretation). The objective tests usually contain many questions with a scale of possible answers to choose from.

Tip: if you can find out what test is being used, then seek additional information about it from the Internet.

Physical Tests

Some occupations may require minimum physical abilities, such as strength, endurance, or speed (e.g. armed forces, police, fire and rescue services).

Tip: investigate what is required by way of testing, and practise the activity to get fit!

A pre-employment medical may also be required, and positions offered may be subject to medical assessment. This may be either a complete medical examination by a medical practitioner or only a questionnaire and declaration form. Be aware that some health-related jobs may also require proof of immunity or vaccinations against certain diseases.

Psychological Tests (Psychometric Tests)

These tests give a standardised way of measuring certain attributes or features of mental behaviour. They include personality and aptitude tests, where the aim is to provide a behavioural profile. Employers will be looking also for indicators of honesty due to the high cost of theft in the industry. They may be seeking team player orientation, problem-solving abilities, independence, and other relevant work attributes.

Tests are standardised through having set questions and a set procedure for administering and scoring the test. It is usually expected that all questions will be answered. However, there are some tests where this is not true as questions get more difficult as you progress. These tests mark on results for completed questions and judge the degree of difficulty from where you finish. The good news is that some of these tests can give you a top score even if not completed! Test questions are usually seeking behavioural responses to set conditions.

Tip: remember that the way you behave at work and home (personal life) may be different, and thus answer from the required work behaviour context.

Skills or Aptitude Tests

Skills tests can be useful to compare what you claim in writing about your abilities with the actual performance of those skills. Not all job applicants are truthful about their abilities! Aptitude tests usually focus on your potential to learn the required skills (e.g. verbal reasoning test). Both test types can also be useful when several candidates appear suitable, and the selection process needs to identify the best in particular talents. Many tests are formatted as multiple-choice questions, and some may get harder as they progress. In the latter case, there may be more value on how far you progress in the test than the expectation that all questions will be answered. Generally though, all questions are scored the same.

If you need to be able to think fast on your feet like a salesperson, then a good test is usually to 'sell' something to the interviewer. Numerical ability may be assessed either verbally or via a written test by providing a set of mathematical problems to solve. This may range from simple addition to analysing scenarios depending on the requirements of the work. An example of this type of test is the numerical reasoning test.

Other ability tests may include:

- abstract thinking (e.g. ability to analyse a problem presented in a visual way)
- lateral thinking (e.g. abstract-reasoning test)
- dexterity (e.g. for fine manual handling)
- mechanical (e.g. mechanical-reasoning test)
- perceptual (e.g. dealing with diagrammatic or symbolic information)
- verbal communication skills
- visual (e.g. colour blindness, night vision)
- spatial (e.g. ability to picture and manipulate shapes mentally)
- typing tests (may be employed to assess speed, accuracy, and correct formatting).

One or more tests may be used to test an applicant's current skills or their future potential.

Other Tests

- attainment—measures your level of learning
- abilities—e.g. numeracy (test may allow the use of a calculator)
- interests—measure what activities you like (employer can make assumptions about work satisfaction)
- integrity tests—measure honesty
- motivations—to discover what drives you to succeed or if indeed you are a motivated person (this may help with more-suitable work placements)
- personnel selection tests—measure desired psychological behaviours but may also identify potential alcohol or substance abuse

- team role—Belbin team role profile (www.belbin.com) is commonly used to judge what type of person you are and thus determine whether your role type is needed in a particular work team—e.g. a person who can initiate new ideas (plant) or a person who is good at finishing off tasks (completer/finisher)
- values—measures what you think is important in life.

Tip: As part of your interview preparation, identify whether the employer has a published set of values (value statement). At times, these may appear in job description statements or promotional literature. This can give clues on what to say at the interview.

How to Prepare for Tests

Test results can be used either to screen applicants for the next stage or to provide points of discussion in the interview. The choice of applicant may be based upon their total score or a set benchmark where all applicants who score above that mark are considered for an interview.

Personality is made up of various traits or dimensions, such as introvert or extrovert, and as such, tests may map out how far along a dimension you score. Depending on the job requirements, the employer may thus select applicants with stronger scores in particular dimensions.

You will not always know what the employer is seeking in a new employee as they may need somebody to fit a specific team profile (Belbin team role profile test).

Tip: It is thus best to be honest in such tests as they are used to determine if you will fit into the job well. A poor fit means that you will not be happy (nor will the employer) and will probably waste time that could have been spent in a more suitable job.

Although employers will have personal biases, the tests overcome that to some extent as they are unbiased. They can thus support your potential to do the job well even if you lack in experience.

The employer may organise a group test where you are amongst others or sit you down on your own. These tests are as important as any you have ever done at school or university, and thus you must pay special attention to all instructions. In particular, identify how to indicate your answers correctly, especially if it is a paper-based test. You may be asked to tick, circle, colour in, etc., and this is often done for a special reason. That is because there may be a method used to scan or score using a device that may misread answers that are not completed correctly. Imagine how you would feel if you failed at this point due to simply being careless!

Another trap is in skipping questions to return to later and then indicating your answer on the wrong line.

Tip: Enquire about any likely tests, including their type and name, as this may assist you in researching them before the event. They may even have some practice tests or test guides, but if not, then try searching the Internet for some.

If you have obtained information on tests from hard-copy books or off the Internet, then be aware that there may also be different levels of complexity and difficulty available. The employer's actual test may also be modified for their industry or special requirements. However, familiarisation and practice on the same type of test should also assist your preparation as does practice at any practical skills required. Those positions requiring mathematical abilities may also need basic mathematical skills practice (percentages, averages, fractions, etc.).

Remember that there may not always be 'correct' answers in certain tests but familiarisation from practice can help reduce nerves and boost confidence. Some tests will draw upon your experience and past training, but before answering, also consider what the employer is after. It may help to consider how role models at work may act in similar circumstances.

Tip: Review the information provided in the advert, job description, value statements, and culture to gain other insights into the desired behaviours. These strategies may help you to identify the required response.

Consider each question carefully even if it states to put down your first thoughts. Skip difficult questions initially. Use all your available time to check and recheck your responses. Do not leave unanswered questions as even a guess may hit the mark and score needed points. Watch out for the same question worded in different ways later in the test to check if you answered consistently.

Tip: if you are experiencing pre-test nerves, then consider following the advice given on reducing interview nerves and stress found later in this book.

Seeking feedback after the test is always worthwhile, but it is often not given. Although you may not have your real paper returned, you may still gain some useful information and advice.

In summary, this pre-interview or testing practice is about providing you with a competitive edge.

Section 2

Preparing for Interviews

Handling the Invitation to an Interview

Getting Chosen for an Interview

Most vacancies have a high number of job applicants, making them very competitive. Applicants may include those already in jobs who are seeking something better or more convenient. This is usually described as a 'buyers' market' for employers. If, on the other hand, you are in a highly sought-after occupation, then you may be approached by a headhunter or an agency.

Tip: Be amongst the first to respond to show your enthusiasm and organisational abilities. At times, the selection process will terminate as soon as a suitable candidate is found.

When employers involve recruitment or employment agencies to screen candidates, the whole process can be prolonged. You may need to meet them, possibly do some tests, and prove you are a worthy candidate to later take up the employer's time at the interview.

Responding to the Invitation

An invitation to attend an interview is usually by phone, but a written request is possible when time is less of an issue. The caller may be an administrative staff member or could be the actual employer. Hence, it is important to answer politely and professionally. Don't be overly emotional over the phone as it may indicate a lack of self-confidence (e.g. you didn't expect to get an interview).

If you were unavailable when the employer called and they left a message, then respond as soon as possible. Be wary that message services that convert voice to a text message are not always reliable. It is recommended that you use a number that has either an answering machine or voicemail service.

Tip: If you have an answering machine or voicemail with a message that may not be appropriate for the potential employer to hear, change it—at least until you have secured the job!

Always find out where, when, and who will be conducting the interviews (and how to pronounce their names!) and repeat this back to ensure you have heard correctly. Also ask whether they would like you to bring anything to the interview (e.g. certain job roles may need portfolios of evidence or past work examples).

If the invitation is by mail, then check for all the details, and phone in to clarify anything not included.

Tip: write a short and concise letter of thanks and intent to attend if there is enough time for the mail; otherwise, send a professionally worded email, or call to confirm.

They will appreciate a quick confirmation so they can lock in their appointments. Ensure you confirm acceptance well before any deadline and ensure you quote the job reference number.

Negotiating Interview Times

You will usually be asked to attend an interview on a set date and time, but occasionally, a choice will be given. When negotiating your attendance at an interview, try to be flexible and ensure your appointment diary is available.

Consider what is more important to you when agreeing to a time that may conflict with another activity. If you argue too much about time, it will appear that you do not have a great commitment to the job, and that leaves a bad impression before you even start! There is no harm in asking if another time is available if you are really pressed for time on the day they are offering. Otherwise, accept the appointment and then work out how to deal with any other commitments later.

Tip: remember, if you want something bad enough, you will be prepared to compromise and look flexible.

Leave adequate time for interviews with different employers that you accept on the same day, and even consider attempting to negotiate interview dates where you can reduce travel in any one day. The last thing you want to do is turn up late at the next interview as you left insufficient time in your schedule.

Pre-interview Research

The Importance of a Job Description

Examine the job description in the advert or an attached document if available online. Request a copy if one is not found. The required document usually includes work duties, responsibilities, reporting lines, and any selection criteria. These may be included on what is described as a job duty statement (JDS), job description form (JDF), person specification, or may be called a job specification form (JSF). In addition, they may include conditions of employment, and there may also be value statements on the form which provide more information about the organisation and what they seek. Often the information contained in these documents is more detailed than the job advert and thus may enlighten you further as to your ability to do the work or make you choose not to proceed.

Tip: Never make the assumption that you are not competitive. If you meet the criteria, go for it!

Some adverts make jobs look more glamorous than they really are. Other adverts may be a trap for the unwary in obtaining payments from you to get into a particular business or make offers that are too good to be true (e.g. promises of potentially high returns/wages).

Tip: Look into such offers very carefully and especially the work conditions as they may be poor and thus warrant the higher wages to

compensate. Be very wary of any requests for an upfront payment prior to acceptance to the next step as scams have been known to occur.

Investigating the Actual Job

Try to find out as much about the job as possible prior to the interview. This will show initiative and resourcefulness and also gives clues about which skills and attributes are important to emphasise at interview. You may also find out that you do not like the work after all and thus may choose to withdraw prior to interview!

Tip: Do not become a no-show at interview but be considerate enough to let them know if you are not attending. Don't burn your bridges for later opportunities.

When researching the job, identify the correct job title, the main functions, key tasks, and required knowledge and skills. Also ask about any special requirements for the job, such as working out of hours or special clothing. If the advert didn't indicate the terms and conditions of employment, you may ask that also, especially for jobs not covered by standard industry award conditions. For example, research salary ranges and conditions for the job by checking other adverts or discussing with the Human Resources (Personnel) Section, employment officer, or personnel manager. This is not an area that you would openly negotiate at an initial interview but would usually save for negotiating when an offer is made. You will read more about this later.

Tip: if you are considering negotiating salary later, then it is obviously helpful to know what others are being paid for similar jobs!

What Can You Find Out about the Company?

Depending on the type of work you are applying for, you may need to research the industry, the company, or the organisation. This may be done through general reading of newspaper articles, business magazines, company annual reports, company websites, professional websites, or public-relations materials available from the business. Internet-based research may also include business Facebook pages, LinkedIn, Twitter, Google News, Google Plus, and other relevant contemporary media.

Tip: Try to research their reputation or image. It is good to understand something of the corporate culture both for your own confidence in wishing to work there and to gain clues that may help with your answers.

You may also obtain clues as to what they like from vision, mission, and values statements. The Human Resources (Personnel), Public Relations, Customer Service, and Marketing or Advertising departments of larger organisations may help you in obtaining these.

A call to the person managing the job enquiries or the person in charge of the area of the vacancy may yield further information on the business.

Tip: You may even ask the person you are speaking to how they enjoy working for the company to gather some in-house information. Be cautious in that some adverts will state that you must not contact the business in this way but must await the interview.

You may even visit the worksite and observe (with permission) the actual conditions in which the vacant position works and ask staff about the job, work culture, and the people. Are they happy, professional, and engaged—or bored and discourteous? Are the premises organised and tidy? Check notice boards for more insight. As a further strategy, use any personal contacts in the business for more information.

Tip: ask yourself, do you still want to work there?

Depending on the type of industry, you may want to know who their competitors are, what the company does well or does poorly, if they have recently done something considered innovative, industry trends for their growth potential, what makes them unique, what services or products are associated with the business, and their reputation. Usually, there are also trade, industry, or professional magazines available from either bookshops, libraries, or the Net. The business section of newspapers can also run articles on the business.

At the department level, there may be goals, values, policies, and procedure files that may prove useful reading.

Not only may you impress the interview panel with current knowledge of their operations, issues, etc. but will also show greater enthusiasm and interest in the job. It can instil greater confidence in an employer if the person they are offering the job to actually knows about the work and their requirements. They will also think that the person is serious about working there and will thus have a better attitude towards work than somebody else just looking for any work they can get.

Remember that you cannot be complacent about interviews and expect to get the job! It is very competitive, and you need research to impress and demonstrate you are above the rest.

Discover Who Will Interview You

If possible, learn the name(s) of interviewer(s), correct pronunciation, and correct title(s) to use. Alternatively, listen carefully on the day of the interview when you are introduced, or if you are lucky, you may be given a business card.

You may even discover their questioning type or other information on their likes or dislikes. This may come from associates who know them well or others who may have been interviewed by them. Panels are usually recommended to comprise both genders (to avoid bias due to personal attraction) and to be an odd number so that a deadlock doesn't occur in making the decision. These recommendations most often occur with public-sector job panels, whereas there is less regulation in private industry and just the manager or supervisor may do the interviews. For higher-level positions, there may be much-larger panels and a longer process.

Tip: consider researching the panel members on LinkedIn (like Facebook for professionals) by checking their profiles for suitable background and interests.

Through your research, you may gain some insight on what aspects to promote in your answers or perhaps simply use the background to establish a quicker positive relationship with the interviewer(s).

Pre-interview Preparation and Practice

Getting Organised

You may possibly attend a number of job interviews before getting the job you want. In order to get organised and learn from your attempts, you should set up a schedule and recording system. This is particularly important if you are out of work and about to tackle many job opportunities. It is probably not necessary if you are only applying for limited job adverts.

You can set up a list or a register with the relevant job name and contact details and leave a column for interview dates and times. Using a personal diary or a smartphone diary may also be helpful. This may help in not making double bookings and keeping track of which job you will be going for on which day. You may even use your register as a record of calls made, jobs applied for, interviews granted, and comments on the interview feedback. More on this later.

Tip: keep a filing system of job adverts and your applications for future reference.

If you are telephoning for the selection criteria or to ask about the work, make sure you can quote the job name, job number (if supplied), and where and when you sourced the advert. This will help the person at the other end as they may be currently advertising a number of jobs.

Interview Planning

Review your invitation to interview (if written) to ensure nothing has been overlooked. Know where you are going for the interview, which route you will take, where you are going to park, public-transport options, and how long it will take to get there. Allow for traffic hold-ups.

Tip: Consider a practice run to see how long it takes and where to park. However, take into account extra the time requirements in peak hours!

Plan what you will wear and what you will take with you. Know the name and title of the person to whom you will report.

If the travel costs or resources are an issue, then consider approaching a government-sponsored job help agency to explore what assistance is available. People with mobility problems or disabilities may also need to explore options to expedite their attendance. Organisations representing people with different disabilities may be able to help. Although employers have obligations under various disability acts to make reasonable adjustments in the workplace, it is not always feasible to do so. Hence, there may be some investigation required to confirm your ability to work in that environment.

Prepare Your Thinking and Potential Responses

Consider your skills, personal attributes, strengths and weaknesses, knowledge base, and what you can accomplish at work. You may be assisted in this process by thinking of things you like and dislike doing. These often correlate with what you do well or do poorly. Think about physical abilities, intellectual abilities, and practical skills.

Tip: Make a list of the above-mentioned factors. Reflection on what you can offer is also motivating and builds self-confidence.

Consider the elements of the work against your own skills and experience. Consider experiences you can relate as evidence of your abilities, if requested. This should include examples of good and bad outcomes. It is permissible to admit to a mistake, but be prepared to follow up with a positive learning outcome and the development of new skills as a consequence. Prepare to relate some success stories.

Tip: Before continuing, consider a reality check! Are you actually qualified for the job? Do you actually want it, or is it more of what you dislike?

If you are committed to wanting the job, then prepare a story on why you are the best person for the job and also why you want the job. More guidelines on what to say are found in the common-questions section later in the book. Rehearse key messages you want to convey about your abilities.

Tip: Be prepared to talk about yourself and your outside interests but avoid sounding too arrogant with strongly worded positive attributes (e.g. describing yourself with words such as 'brilliant' or 'exceptional' may sound too strong). Your prepared response should be less than two minutes long.

Consider your own career goals as sometimes you will be asked, particularly with respect to your plans for the next five years. Refer to the later section on common questions for further guidance on this.

Consider answers to possible questions but do not practise rote answers. Instead, remember key points to discuss. You may write these key points on index cards, and then you may be allowed to take them into the interview to refer to, only if needed. If you plan and practise perfect answers only, then an unexpected question may also put you off balance or cause you to go blank. When criteria are involved, be prepared with questions that may merge two or more criteria (e.g. there may be criteria on communication skills, interpersonal skills, and teamwork). All three can be interrelated, so also consider questions such as how communications can affect teamwork.

Next, consider some goals for the interview. These may include what you want to get across and also what you want answered. If the interview questions do not bring out your strengths satisfactorily, then find a way to include a statement about them before you leave.

How to Practise for an Interview

The interview is similar to a performance on stage, and as such, rehearsals are important before the big event. Adopt a confident style and clearly articulate your responses. Try to categorise your answers rather than just say what comes off the top of your head.

Try to give a structured and logical answer, possibly in point form so that you appear organised in your thinking. Structure can be easily applied to answering some questions, and that will help you to remember key points with a probability of gaining more points from the panel.

For example, consider selection criteria on teamwork and what makes you a good team player. Answer from the perspective of commencing in a new position. In an introductory period, you would meet other team members, learn of their roles and how they interact, and learn what is expected from you in your work and communications. You would then move into the integration phase, where you become an integral and efficient member of the team, sharing workloads, timing work around and with others, and participating in social activities. Then you move into a mature phase, where you can guide or mentor newer members of the team, recognise when others need your emotional or psychological support, and provide leadership when called upon.

Another example may be in managing your time. In your response, you would firstly consider the demand on your time by identifying new and previous work demands along with required attendance at meetings. You would then go through the process of prioritisation in your day, outlining tasks by importance and urgency—in other words, how you expect to meet the demand identified, including how any unexpected events would require a revision. You would outline any strategies for minimising work interruptions. Next, you can describe how you would also take actions in accord with longer-term goals (e.g. weekly, placement, annual work, or self-development goals). If they are not monitored and don't have a plan of action, then they will probably not be achieved.

For questions requiring past examples, a suitable framework to help in organising your answer is helpful as previously mentioned in the book:

- SAO stands for outlining the *situation*, then the *action* you took, and finally the *outcome*.
- STAR technique is another similar framework. This stands for the *situation*, the *task* you had to perform to address the situation, the *actions* you took (what and how), and the *results*.

Using either technique will help you think through a logically presented answer.

Practise going through the interview in one of a number of ways:

- Use your imagination (visualisation technique). Read more on this under the 'Points to Reduce Interview Stress or Nerves' section.
- Practise with a friend who can ask their own questions or use yours.
- Record some questions and practise answering.
- Audio-record or video yourself to listen and watch your expression, and try to sound enthusiastic and not monotonous or bored.
- Hold mock interviews with a consultant.

What to Bring

Bring copies of your résumé or CV (one for each panel member and one for you to refer to), references, academic records, portfolio (if relevant), notepad, and two pens to the interview. Keep your papers together in a presentable folder or display book, not loosely as they are likely to fall at some stage. Store them in a display book in a logical, ordered fashion, which makes documents easy to find. You may even have testimonials, press reports, in-house awards, etc. that you may bring to show your accomplishments.

Tip: It is sound advice not to leave any original documents, or you may not see them again. Instead, request a copy to be made straight away or, better still, provide a spare copy.

Carry details of the interviewer's name and contact number in your mobile phone in case of delay caused by unexpected traffic issues. Have referee details available if requested. Consider taking a water bottle and any last-minute grooming aids (e.g. nail file) that you may need on the day.

It may also look impressive to bring some information on the business and will demonstrate that you have taken the job seriously and shown interest in learning about the business.

Points to Ponder for Your Motivation

- If you have been offered an interview, then you already have the interest of the employer.
- If you have been shortlisted, then you know that you look suitable for the job.
- Many of the questions are predictable and thus may be practised. Refer to the sample lists later.

Preparing for Poor Interviewers

Prepare your expectations about the fact that not all interviewers are good at what they do. Their behaviours may include being rude, biased, sexist, and displaying poor communication skills. They may look totally disorganised by being late, not having your details on hand, being unsure of the job you are being interviewed for, allowing frequent interruptions, being poor at timekeeping, etc.

In addition, not all interview rooms are the same, and it could prove large or small, noisy and distracting, or with furniture creating barriers between you and the interviewers.

How you manage the situation will be determined by how much you desire the job and how good you are at keeping calm and in control.

Tip: refer also to the later section on 'Dealing with the Bad Interviewer' for strategies to employ at the actual interview.

The Ninety-Day Action Plan

You may receive a question about what you would do if appointed to the job, and thus it is recommended that you prepare a ninety-day action plan. This will impress them on your apparent organisational ability, motivation to do well, and ambition.

Basically, you consider a plan of action and attainments for each thirty days up to the end of ninety days, or three months. Be prepared to be flexible if some of their plans for you appear to conflict with your plan. It is best to consider the following areas and choose those of most relevance.

Get to know the company, reporting structures, values, strategic plans, and working relationships as part of your induction period. This should include actions to gain acceptance within the team. Consider what you will do to become a good team player. You will expect to progress over the ninety days from a learning period to being fully aware of all job requirements and then to being fully integrated into the business.

Over the course of the period, you will learn of any job performance expectations and appraisal systems, moving from clarifying expectations to demonstrating competence and then to working at a consistent standard.

Technical abilities and knowledge will progress from understanding to becoming proficient and then to developing recognised expertise. Safety issues are also important to focus on early.

Tip: Show some respect for the work by not being over optimistic or arrogant about becoming an expert too soon if such attainment is not realistic for that job within that time frame!

Personal development in the role will progress from taking directions to ensuring you are on the right track and to ultimately being confident in your abilities.

Points to Reduce Interview Stress or Nerves

Points to Ponder

It should be noted that some nerves or stress is very common for interviews, and in fact, a small amount of stress can help performance. However, emotional, physiological, and behavioural changes can eventuate. People respond in their own ways or patterns and in variable degrees. This may include dry mouth, excessive sweatiness, rapid pulse, shakes, red blotches, stammering, rambling, forgetfulness, poor concentration, clumsiness, and stomach pains. A person may also exhibit nervous mannerisms, such as fidgeting, biting nails, biting lips, and scratching. There may also be habits that irritate others (e.g. twirling hair around a finger); all these should be recognised, and one should have strategies developed to reduce them on the day—or forever!

To be successful at interviews, it is advisable that you should be in an alert state of mind and be reasonably relaxed. It is also helpful if you have practised avoiding negative self-talk and feelings. For example, don't reflect on past unsuccessful interviews at that time, but consider each new interview as an opportunity to shine. In fact, see it as your chance to interview the employer, and feel good about the fact that you have presented yourself well enough to get an interview. The interviewer wants you to succeed as they want to find a solution to their problem of a job vacancy. A good interviewer should help you to relax on arrival in the room. However, this is not always the case, so you must consider other strategies.

Tip: Bear in mind that questions may also be included at an interview on whether you have stress at work and how you cope. Refer to the sample questions in the final section of this book for ideas on what they may ask and a pointer on how to answer.

Strategies to Reduce Stress

The first step in reducing stress is with thorough interview preparation. The more you research and know about the job, practise for the interview, and control negative stress-inducing thoughts, the better. Try the following strategies:

- Practise the interview as described previously.
- Attend a number of interviews to gain confidence.
- Practise your answers to the most common questions. Keep in mind that 'failing' in one question does not necessarily mean that you won't get the job. Therefore, don't allow yourself to give in at that point, and keep performing.
- Don't read through your notes again while in the waiting area if it makes you more nervous.
- Prepare a response should you show your nerves. Try using some humour about it, and state that your nerves are a reflection on how seriously you feel about the job.
- Build your self-confidence by reflecting on your work successes to date and all that you are offering as an employee.
- Avoid negative self-talk on the day of the interview, such as 'I should have done . . .', 'I know I will stuff something up!', and 'I am terrible at interviews!' If you discover that you are thinking these types of thoughts, try to cease and switch to positive, motivating ones. Celebrate the fact that you have followed the strategies outlined in this book and you have thus prepared well.
- Listen to music that helps you relax while on the way to the interview, but if driving, still remain alert.

- Work on getting some relaxation time (e.g. have a massage, do some meditation, exercise, practise progressive muscular-relaxation technique). Try quick relaxation techniques while waiting to go into the interview. For example, you could sit in a comfortable position, try a few slow, deep breaths down to the diaphragm and not just the upper chest, and end with a smile. This is often enough to rest your nerves and provide some calm. Remember to take the occasional deeper breath in the interview also.
- Try a meditation visualisation technique—not just once, but on a number of occasions! For example, after relaxing in a place free of interruption with your mobile phone off, close your eyes and then imagine—as if looking through your own eyes—going into the building for the interview, then talking to the receptionist and, after maybe waiting a short time, being shown to the interview room. See yourself meeting the panel and using a positive and firm handshake, then sitting down and feeling relaxed but alert, confident, and calm. Imagine the whole process going well and that you're feeling good about the people and your performance, later thanking the interviewer and travelling home, feeling confident. Feel the emotions attached to success. Practise several scenes. Ignore irrelevant or distracting thoughts, and refocus. After a while, the whole interview will seem like déjà vu, which means it is like you have done it already and it, therefore, no longer troubles you.
- Another method to use is affirmations, which are positive, goal-oriented statements that are motivating and are expressed as if something desired has already been attained. For example, you make up a series of statements such as 'I am relaxed and confident at interviews'. Write them down and refer to them frequently, but when doing so, you must believe in what you say and feel the emotion as well. It is not good enough to write 'I wish to be comfortable at interviews' as this is a wish and is always something not yet attained. You must phrase the affirmation as if it is already true for it to work. You can use a combination of these with the visualisation technique mentioned above in the one session. The complete meditative session need not take longer than ten minutes at a time.

- Do not take sedatives or alcohol prior to the interview as this can be disastrous in slowing and distorting the thinking and leaving the wrong impression.
- Consider hypnosis to overcome interview nerves, stress, and anxiety. It is best done one on one with a hypnotherapist to be most effective as the sessions can be tailored to you as an individual. Alternative methods include hypnosis CDs or MP3s that include the particular subject and can be listened to on many occasions to reinforce the message. They may include subliminal messages designed to reinforce the message.
- If you continue to experience extreme stress and anxiety, then consider seeing a psychologist for additional strategies.
- At the end of the day, remember that other opportunities will arise and you learn from each opportunity.

Planning for Success on the Day

Aim to arrive at least fifteen minutes early as a buffer against unforeseen circumstances and to allow yourself to settle down a little. You won't make a good impression if you present yourself as puffed and sweating from rushing! Plan on some time to relax and gather your thoughts before your appointment time. Arriving too early and announcing your arrival may lead to pressure on the interviewer to see you early, and you don't want to begin by annoying them! Some small businesses only have limited space to seat waiting interviewees, so ten minutes early is probably enough. Practise calming techniques while you wait.

If an emergency or illness arises on the day of the interview and you can't attend or will be late, then you must notify the panel and ask for a reschedule of your interview. Sleeping in and missing the interview is not an option! If you are unable to phone through, ask somebody else to do so, and the panel will appreciate the warning.

Personal Factors

On the previous evening or the day of the interview, you should avoid meals and beverages that may cause breath odour (e.g. garlic, strong fish, or heavy alcohol). Alcohol on the day will dull your senses. Smoking on the day may make you smell unpleasant to members of the panel. A heavy meal on the day may make you feel uncomfortable or sleepy. Ensure sufficient sleep the night prior in order to help with good energy levels at the interview. Avoid sleeping pills as they may have a carry-over effect into the next day. Personal hygiene is also important (e.g. control of body odour). Don't overdo the perfume or aftershave so that, in a closed room, it is hard to breathe! Keep your sweaty hands dry for the handshake when meeting the interviewer(s).

Should I Bring Somebody with Me?

If you are a school applicant, then consider the impression that having your parents present may make on the employer. It does not engender confidence in you as an employee as you will require a degree of independence when at work. Work conditions and contracts can always be checked later by family members before signing up.

Adult applicants may appear too dependent or lacking in confidence if they are seen with accompanied by others in the waiting area.

Why Are Image and Presentation Vital?

First impressions do count! Impressive presentations can potentially help you beat other applicants who are more qualified or experienced than you.

People form an opinion on you within the first thirty seconds of contact, so don't let them develop the wrong impression. Generally, it is within the first four minutes of an interview that first impressions are consolidated. It could mean the difference between getting and losing that job! The interviewer will quickly determine whether you meet the required standards and values of their workplace and whether you will fit in with other employees. If they like what they see, it can diminish other shortcomings in your assessment, which is often referred to as the halo effect. Dressing appropriately will thus earn early respect from the employer.

It can be important to maintain a good image with the receptionist as their opinion may be sought in some cases.

You have probably heard the saying 'You can't judge a book by its cover', but the fact is that most people do!

The image you project is a combination of the clothes you wear, your personal grooming, body language (e.g. posture or the way you walk—so walk tall by standing straight and not slouching), and the way you talk. If you present poor grooming habits, which indicate lazy or indifferent attitudes, then the employer may believe that you will carry out your work in the same way. Poor habit indicators may include unpolished shoes, unclean fingernails, uncombed messy hair, body odour, dirty or unironed clothes, and unshaven appearance. There are work cultures that may be less conservative (e.g. fashion or entertainment), so research expectations on appearance before the interview.

Tip: Some of these points may go counter to your generational expectations or street appearance, but consider making an effort to change for the interview. Do you really want the job?

Remember that you must stand out from the rest of the applicants if you want to increase your chances of selection. However, anybody projecting an image that is substandard or at times too flamboyant will simply not get selected. Remember that, in many jobs, the image that staff members portray is very important as it conveys quality, attention to detail, etc. It must align with the corporate image and culture.

What to Wear

Interview applicants may think 'How I look should not make a difference!' or 'I am being employed for my skills, not my looks!' or 'I will wear what I like as it is my ability to do the job that counts!' or 'I like my body piercings, and I am not taking them out for anybody!' In principle, all these thoughts are reasonable with respect to being able to do the work being most important. However, remember you are trying to impress prospective employers who may be conservative, and they will choose whom to employ! If you want the job, be prepared to compromise for it!

Although you may rightfully consider it discriminatory for them to reject you on the basis of your appearance; nevertheless, first impressions are most important. A negative impression may influence, even subconsciously, the way the interviewer will interpret your answers to their questions. Even if the job is not one in which you would be expected to dress smartly or formally, it may still impress the interviewers that you made the effort to dress up for the event.

Looking good will increase your self-confidence, and that always helps with performance at the interview. Wearing cosmetics for women is associated with success in employment. Consider free help from make-up consultants in department stores about the use of their product, but be aware that they are not necessarily image consultants also. That is a different skill. It is recommended that you consult a beautician, image consultant, or hairdresser for professional advice on improving your personal image as it is beyond the scope of this book.

In deciding what clothing to wear, you may seek advice from clothing stockists or image consultants. Don't think that you have to go and buy a whole new expensive wardrobe. Appropriate attire can vary from industry to industry and position to position.

Tip: As a strategy, consider observing the style of dress (dress code) that people wear in the relevant business or industry. Try a walk-and-observe tour (i.e. observe what people wear at that workplace by dropping in at lunchtime or closing time when people are circulating). Of course, if you already know somebody working there, check with them about appropriate clothes to the interview.

Clothing should not be so bright and complex as to distract the interviewer from what you are saying. Generally, dress at least one level above the position you are applying for. Wearing a suit can impress the employer but is not essential unless it goes with that type of job. Consider smart clothing as an alternative to a suit, but this will be determined by the nature and level of job you may be applying for. For example, a person applying for a physically demanding job would not be expected to show up for the interview in a suit, whereas a person applying for an office position would usually need one.

If you are going to school at the time of interviews, then it is best to change out of school clothes into something more like you would wear to a job. If you have to go straight from school, then at least try to smarten up a little and put on a school blazer if you have one.

Tip: Consider what to wear prior to the interview day and check if it is in good order—including zips, buttons, and fly—and working! You don't want to experience stress on the day by repairing clothing!

Presentation tips may include:

- Dress conservatively in coordinated style and colour.
- Males should consider a suit in conservative colours for professional, office, management jobs, etc. (consider hiring, but do not try to upstage the boss!) or smart clothing if a suit seems overdressed. Avoid flat black, but consider blues and greys, and ensure they are well fitting.
- Trousers should be at just over heel length at the back and should cover approximately a third of the shoe length in front.
- Belts usually match the shoe colour, but avoid inappropriate buckles that could bias or fail to impress the interviewer.
- Men's shirts should be long-sleeved and usually a white or pale colour. They should fit properly with the right sleeve length.
- Avoid joke, cartoon, symbols, or branded ties. Silk or silk-blend ties usually wear well. It should complement the suit but not match it in the exact same colour. The length should reach your belt when standing.
- Shoes should be worn rather than joggers or sports shoes, thongs, or sandals unless culturally accepted or appropriate to the job. Leather shoes, either black or brown, should be polished and clean.
- Socks should also be in complementary colours, and as with ties, avoid joke socks as they show when seated.
- Women's suits or business dresses with matching jackets need to be guided by current fashions but be well fitting and finished. Seek guidance on this as fashion advice in a book quickly becomes out of date.
- Avoid miniskirts, revealing skirts with leg slits, low-cut revealing blouses, etc.

- Blouses should not have gaping buttons over the chest. Long sleeves are best for that professional image. Light colours are popular choices, but be wary of fabrics that show perspiration from nerves.
- Scarves can be acceptable, but similar to men's ties, they should complement the outfit and should not be too flamboyant.
- Women's shoes have a greater variety than males and should work within the colour scheme of the dress or trousers. Try to stay with the professional look unless the job class demands greater style and individuality.
- Handbags should not be oversized or too baggy.
- Clothing generally should not be old-looking, frayed, holed, dirty, or overly sexy.
- Cosmetics should be appropriate to the situation—not necessarily the same as preparing for an evening out.
- Do not overdo perfume, scented hairspray, or aftershave.
- Watch out for excess jewellery. The focus should be on you at the interview and interviewers should not be too distracted elsewhere.
- Try to cover tattoos.
- Have a good haircut or at least tidy hair (washed and no dandruff) and beards or moustaches neatly trimmed. Avoid hair obscuring the eyes. Avoid cuts that constantly need attention during the interview as it can become annoying to watch.
- Spectacles should be clean and fit straight. Do not wear sunglasses as they hide the eyes.
- Use deodorant as nerves can make you sweaty, and pay attention to dental hygiene and breath.
- Trim and clean your nails, and for women, use a conservative colour of nail polish.

Tip: Finally, try the bathroom mirror test. Stand in front of the mirror and ask yourself, 'Based on what you see, would you employ this person?' Remember to check the rear side also for things that are out of place, like tags and hems.

Section 3

The Actual Interview

At the Interview

What to Do if You Are Kept Waiting

If you are kept waiting beyond your appointment time (not arrival time!), then try to remain calm and use the time to further your preparation. There may be some reports or other documents available to read, or you may want to review some of your own materials. Alternatively, practise some of your calming or interview preparation techniques mentioned previously. When finally met, do not complain! If the person says sorry to have kept you waiting, then be gracious and say 'That is OK' or 'No problem'. To make a greater impression, if you had used the wait time in further preparation, then you can say something about how you found the delay useful or 'I was able to use the delay to good effect'.

Tip: Remember to be polite to the waiting-area staff as they too may pass on their impressions. Be on your best behaviour with any other employees you meet also as they may be future colleagues or supervisors!

Proceeding to the Interview

When you first arrive, you can expect to wait until called into the interview room. Turn your mobile phone off, preferably or at least to meeting or silent mode if an expected call is more important than the interview! Remember, you need to give your undivided attention to the panel during the interview! You will usually be met by one of the panel, usually the chairperson, but may also be taken to the room by the secretary/receptionist or another panel member.

If you are shown to the door of the interview room and it is shut, knock and wait to hear somebody say enter. Do not just barge in, but when invited, walk in confidently. Shut the door quietly behind you, preferably without turning your back on the interviewer(s). Once in the room, you will be presented to any other panel members usually while still standing.

Approach the interviewer(s), and smile while meeting and shaking hands. Handshakes must be firm, not limp or crushing. Your handshake should thus not be too weak, often described as like a 'dead fish', nor should it be so strong that the other person feels like they are being crushed or in a contest! Try to match the other party where possible. Remember that, in Western culture, a limp handshaker appears less confident, less trustworthy, and less genuine in their greeting. Try to keep your hands dry and warm for the handshake. Maintain eye contact while shaking hands and give a friendly smile.

The shake usually lasts only a second or two and should not be too vigorous. The hand is offered in a vertical position. Don't shirt-front them by standing too close during the shake! If you are unsure about the handshake length or grip, then get some opinions before the day and get it right. People will not tell you unless you ask. Generally, both men and women shake hands. However, be sensitive to any cultural restrictions with body and eye contact.

Using the interviewer's correct name when addressing them in greeting will usually impress. Use the first name only when invited or otherwise seems appropriate, but this depends on the business culture. First names are often used in corporate interviews and meetings.

Tip: One way to help you remember names is to repeat the person's name when responding to the introduction. Another way is to make a quick note on sitting down.

It is generally expected that you will wait until told where and when to sit. Place any bags on the floor and not on your lap. This will avoid dropping them during the interview and also make you look less nervous than if clutching a bag to your lap. Keep important papers and pens handily placed.

Structure of the Interview

The person in charge will usually begin some small talk to break the ice and attempt to get you a little more relaxed before beginning the serious questions. Look for opportunities to impress on your preparation and research (e.g. small talk may include a question about the traffic or ease of finding the site). Then you may respond by saying that you had no problems because you checked parking out when dropping in the other day to obtain a copy of the company's annual report. Weather may be a common opener. Talk on bad weather should not be overly long, but turn this to a positive by pointing out how you get on with enjoying life irrespective of the weather.

Avoid answers that are long or too personal in this preamble. You may initiate some of the small talk based on something seen in the room or the building (e.g. hobbies, interests displayed around the room, or maybe about works going on). However, like most general advice, try to avoid conflict arising from opposing points of view held on politics or religion in particular.

You may be offered a drink (water) at this stage (good for dry mouth from nerves), and usually, the structure of the session may be explained (especially if in the public sector).

Questions may begin with recent work experience and clarifying previous job details or other material in your written application. If this is for your first job, then the focus may be on school or university activities and achievements.

This will usually be followed by questions appropriate to the job, and then later will be a time for you to ask questions and/or say anything further in support of your application. Use this time wisely. Refer to a later section on questions you can ask. You should have your prepared two-minute statement ready as a final summary of your value and commitment to the job.

Facts about Interviews

It is essential to make a positive first impression as interviewers typically judge you in the opening minutes of the interview. Your appearance and behaviour all play a role as discussed in a previous section.

It is recommended that you make your most important statements at the beginning and end of the interview. This is because many people tend to pay less attention in the middle phase of the discussion. In other words, make good use of any opportunity to make an opening statement and closing statement. The opening statement may be in response to a question on why you have applied or what you can offer if employed.

Using negative statements or complaints in your dialogue are more likely to influence the interviewer against you than if you focus on positive reasons and examples. Consider the difference between 'I am leaving my last job because I couldn't stand the boss' versus 'I am seeking a new job that will utilise all the skills I have developed'. Thus your pre-interview preparation must include consideration of how to respond to such questions.

Uncovering the Hidden Criteria

You may be able to uncover clues as to what the interviewers are looking for in the desired applicant. Formal job descriptions may not always spell out what they are really seeking in the perfect employee. It is best to discover this before answering any important questions. Hence, get in early and break the ice after introductions are complete but without seeming too pushy! This may not always be possible if the interview is tightly controlled, but if the opportunity presents itself, you can then ask, 'Before we proceed, I am curious as to how you would describe the ideal candidate for this job.'

If they list a number of attributes and skills, then ask which would be the more important. Also try to uncover more of the duties if the information researched before the interview was not clear enough. By discovering all this information early in the interview, you can emphasise skills and examples that they want to hear.

Improving on Speech and Language

Your voice may lead to wrong impressions or annoy the panel. Consider recording and hearing how you sound when answering practice questions. Get feedback from a friend and encourage them to be honest with you. You may, in fact, talk too quietly, too quickly (or ramble), or too loudly, which may be associated with nerves or hearing issues. Practise getting the volume right, though be prepared to speak more quietly or more loudly if the room warrants it. The amount of furnishing and size of the room can make a difference to how easily you are heard.

When talking at interviews, try to avoid the use of slang words (e.g. 'you' instead of 'youse', 'yes' instead of 'yer'), and do not swear.

Tip: do not swear even if the interviewer does, and remain professional.

Avoid slurring your speech or mumbling, and remember to maintain some eye contact with panel members. Watch your enunciation or pronunciation as better pronunciation of words may equate with higher intelligence to some. Don't cover your mouth when you speak. Work on your expression so you can avoid ums and ahs, and watch out for other bad habits like frequently saying 'you know' or 'like'. Record a conversation and listen for your faults. They can be improved once you are aware of them.

Tip: If you need to develop your voice or manner of speaking, then gain some tips from the Internet, or if you need greater help, then consider seeing a speech pathologist (therapist) for appropriate exercises.

Try to speak clearly with a steady voice at an appropriate volume as this will convey confidence. Alternatively, if you hesitate or stumble during your answers, it can appear that you lack confidence, are possibly ill-prepared, or are letting nerves take over. The interviewer should not have to ask you to repeat yourself as this may indicate your volume is too low and thus again showing lack of self-confidence. Use your natural voice, not a false voice as it will show. Try to inject a little confidence and enthusiasm into your voice by varying your pitch, not just a dull monotone or you may present yourself as boring or disinterested. Again, check by recording a mock interview and then listening to how you sound on playback!

Remember not to give answers that are too long-winded, or you will risk annoying the interviewer! Thus, try to be more precise in discussion through better word choice (e.g. consider replacing the phrase 'last but not least' with the word 'finally'). You may use other common phrases that you can reflect on and replace them with more-concise words.

Tip: avoid using tentative language, such as 'I feel I could' or 'I think I can', as this causes doubt in your abilities!

Taking Notes at the Interview

Be prepared for the panel to be taking notes during the interview as they need to be able to compare answers later and possibly score and rank the candidates. This is especially necessary when there are a number of candidates that must be remembered in post-interview decision-making. A good interviewer should be consistent in their note-taking and not just note negatives as this can be very off-putting to the candidate.

Tip: If you notice the panel members are having trouble keeping up with you when writing their notes, consider slowing down. This is not only considerate, but they may miss points that count later when scoring. Conversely, if they stop writing, then you may be off-track.

It is not a good idea for you to take notes at the interview as it can be annoying to the panel and may slow things down. You may limit yourself to writing down quick key points only as an aid to answering the question and thus not forgetting any components to the question. However, if you can manage without this, it is better. Also, it is best to ask at the start if it is permissible for you to take notes. Also clarify what notes you may want to take—e.g. 'I may just write down key points in your questions to ensure I fully answer them. Is that OK?'

Discriminatory Issues

Don't volunteer information that could be subject to discrimination (e.g. marital status, children, religion, sexual orientation, age, political preference). It may subconsciously or otherwise influence their decision. Refer also to the later section on questions that should not be asked.

Listening

Show that you are listening through eye contact, nodding, or affirming verbally, but do not interrupt. Listen to the whole question before considering your reply. Remember not to display poor body language via the posture of inattention or boredom. Show value and interest in what the speaker is saying.

Be aware of the panel member's body language and verbal importance (emphasis) that may be placed on key words in the question. What are they looking for in your answer? Ask them to clarify the question if it seems ambiguous, remembering that, in some structured interviews, they may only repeat the question and not change it.

Smoking

Do not ask to smoke at the interview. There may also be prohibitions to smoking at that worksite.

Monitoring Your Time

It can be important in timed interviews to be aware of how much time remains. You may have a set number of questions and thus need to allow enough time to answer them all. Failure to do so could mean failure at the interview. You could ask for the number of questions at the start of a structured formal interview so you can judge your progress. The panel will thus understand when you are seen checking with your watch. However, constant clock-watching can also suggest that you want the interview to be over or that you have someplace better to be or are simply bored. It is thus important to avoid this practice unless your interview is tightly timed.

Some interviewers provide questions in advance, and if so, it allows you a better appreciation of how long to spend on each question. Try wearing your watch with the face on the palm side of your wrist so it is easily seen without turning your wrist over. This makes it less obvious that you are concerned over your time. If you do not usually wear a watch and use your mobile phone, then perhaps borrow one for the event. Remember that it is recommended that your mobile phone is turned off during the interview.

Reading the Signs

Signs that the interview is going well may include:

- spending longer at the interview than planned
- calling in other people to meet you
- getting down to the details about start dates or salary
- being invited back for a second interview.

Signs that the interview is not going so well may include:

- The interview lasts a shorter time than planned.
- You are not able to answer questions. Remember to prepare for them next time.
- It becomes apparent that the work requirements exceed your skills or abilities.
- The panel members were making notes during the interview but have now stopped. This could show that you are taking too long, off-track, or possibly rambling. Try to refocus by asking if you have said enough or maybe should say more about another aspect of the question. The panel will either say 'You have said enough' or will redirect your answer to the aspect they are looking for.

- The panel members look distracted, tuned out, fidgety, bored, or have stopped talking. On the last point, they could be waiting for you to say more! Hence, silence may indicate 'What else can you add?'
- The panel member frowns during your answer. This is a sure sign that you should immediately reflect on what you just said and change direction or correct a wrong impression.

More on the Importance of Body Language

Body language accounts for about 50 per cent of communication, followed by tone of voice (30 per cent) and the actual words being only about 20 per cent! Hence, it can be crucial to the success of your interview.

Strategies to Influence the Interviewer

Indicate you are listening through slowly nodding occasionally and leaning back in the chair. You may also use other body expressions that demonstrate attentiveness, interest, and understanding, such as nodding, raising your eyebrows, or tilting your head.

Watch the manner you portray yourself (e.g. bored, frustrated, negative, and unfriendly manners will not win you a job). Interviewers on the whole like to choose happy, positive people. Who wants to work with somebody who is always grumbling or complaining? Remember to smile occasionally but not too falsely. Smiling should be real, appropriately used, and not be overdone or constant or it starts to look insincere and annoying.

You need to give the impression of taking the job seriously and being interested, confident, and reliable. Hence, body language is important, and if you are not aware of how different mannerisms are interpreted, then you may give the wrong impression. What you are saying must match your body language, or else you will confuse the interviewer!

The Importance of Eye Contact

Looking at the person when they speak shows interest and attentiveness. Avoid staring though as it is taken as aggressive, and it is normal to break eye contact for short periods. When looking away, it is better to look left or right than down into your lap, which may appear submissive. Try to vary your visual point of reference from eye to eye or their mouth as they talk. In panels, pay attention to the person asking the question but involve all members with eye contact when you are answering.

Try to determine the person with the most influence on the panel, give them proportionately more attention, and try to impress them. Not making eye contact leads to the assumption that the person has something to hide or totally lacks self-confidence. Don't be caught staring blankly at some object in the room as it shows disinterest. Avoid staring at the interviewer's body below the shoulders, especially the opposite sex, as it may give the wrong image!

If you usually wear glasses, do so for the interview. Avoid appearing haughty by peering above the rims at the speaker. Only wear reading glasses when you need them. Avoid hiding eyes behind sunglasses as it makes it hard for the interviewer to judge the veracity of what you are saying (e.g. when speaking a lie, a right-handed person tends to look up to the right). The reverse is true of left-handed people. People also tend to blink more rapidly (eye flutter) or rub their eyes when they lie. This is not 100 per cent accurate, but along with other signs, practised interviewers and interrogators can identify lies. A hairstyle that may obscure one or both eyes may also prove a barrier to good body language.

Watch Out for Annoying Habits

Similar to the previous point about indicators of potential lying, touching your nose and ears, scratching your neck, pulling on your collar, playing with your tie, or placing your hand over your mouth may indicate exaggeration or lying! In other words, try not to hide your face either.

Practise controlling your responses to questions that you do not know the answer to. Hence, avoid pulling a face or shrugging but stay composed and seek more guidance on the question.

Watch out for annoying or nervous habits, such as twirling of hair, fiddling with pens and buttons, gnawing on your lips, or just being too fidgety. Hence, reduce any hand-or-foot movements, and don't keep changing positions in the chair. Become aware of your bad habits and practise not doing them in the interview.

The Importance of Hands and Posture

Sit comfortably in an upright but not slumped or slouched posture, or else you may portray disinterest or laziness. Try to avoid crossing legs or ankles unless necessary.

Lean forward slightly when talking and back when listening. Be subtle about that and not exaggerated, or it will look obvious and unnatural!

Matching (mirroring) postures with the person you are talking to may indicate to them that you are on the same wavelength. However, don't make this too obvious through immediate responses but move gently into the new posture. Watch out that they do not have a peculiar mannerism as mirroring may then appear as making fun of them!

Don't cross your arms or hug something else to your chest—it can indicate aggression, defensiveness, resistance, or a closed mind.

You may use your hands for emphasis or openness (palms upward) or to show you are thinking on something (church steeple position). Otherwise, keep hands in your lap or on the arms of the chair, or if you don't have an interview table, then maybe holding on to papers (in folder) or a notepad. Be cautious not to overdo the hand gestures as you may appear overly anxious.

General Interview Advice

About Being Honest

Don't pretend to be someone you are not as a good interviewer will pick up on the inconsistencies. Note that you will also have to live up to such a false image in the job. Therefore, remember to be honest with yourself because if you get a job that you are not suited for, then you will be unhappy later and will ultimately leave or be dismissed. Your act may also be caught out with probing interview questions that reveal your true nature.

Also, be honest when questioned, but this does not mean that you have to disclose or reveal everything about yourself (dirty laundry). Stick to the point unless it will be in your favour. Remember that lying is often obvious to the experienced communicator.

On Being Likable

Demonstrate a positive and confident (not arrogant) attitude at the interview as employers want people who are positive, energetic, and displays enthusiasm in their work. Similarly, try to be positive in your answers as people do not usually like those who appear negative about everything. You need to present yourself as likable (not in all jobs necessarily) by smiling and laughing when appropriate, projecting a good mood, and using panel members' names appropriately.

Maintain this demeanour even if the interview does not seem to be going well as you must not write yourself off too early. Avoid seeming dull, bored, or defeated.

Avoid being overly familiar by using titles and surnames until told otherwise. This demonstrates respect, though in higher-level positions, it can be more appropriate to use first names, especially if you are being headhunted or have professional skills which are in demand.

Memorising Answers

Apply caution to simply memorising answers as you may not sound convincing and may get caught out if the question asked is slightly different to what has been rehearsed. However, preparing answers to possible questions will enable you to relax more at the interview. By practising different questions, you will develop flexibility to handle the many variations that are possible. Refer to the later practice questions for ideas on what to prepare.

Motivation and Attitude

Treat every interview like it is the only one that you will get, so be hungry for the job. Be prepared to sell yourself and your skills appropriately without sounding too bombastic or maybe overconfident. Apply caution in the area of name-dropping as it can also backfire—for example, if that person is out of favour with the interviewer!

Show the interview panel how you are the solution to their problem (i.e. job vacancy) and try not to leave any doubts about your commitment and ability to do the work.

Strategies on Dealing with Questions

Collect your thoughts before answering. Don't take too long though, and think quietly. Talking to yourself could get annoying. Usually, several seconds are enough, whereas more than that can become uncomfortable to the panel and can place your communication abilities in doubt. However, behavioural-type questions seeking an example from your experience may warrant a longer pause while you consider the best situation to discuss.

Also consider why the panel asked a particular question and what they may be looking for in the answer. Be reasonably concise in your answers, but not just a yes or no! These answers also make it harder on the panel. Avoiding yes or no answers also allows you to take every opportunity to sell yourself to the panel. However, talking for too long and not getting to the point may result in doubt on your communication and time management capabilities. It may also lead to pressure on the panel to meet the interview schedule. If in doubt about whether you have said enough or maybe too much, you could ask, 'Would you like me to say more about . . . ?'

If you do not understand the question, ask that it be rephrased if possible, or seek clarification by asking, 'Do you want me to discuss . . . ?' If you are running out of ideas during the answer time, try asking the panel to repeat the question. Often hearing it again will trigger a new line of thought.

Don't forget to watch their body language for clues that you are off the track or are saying too much. Remember that if the panel members stop writing, it could indicate you are off the point. Take the hint, and check if they want you to continue down that track. This may even get them to indicate if they have heard enough on that question. Avoid just rambling on about nothing (often nerves) or off the point.

Make sure you listen to the question as there may be more than one part or an emphasis may be placed on what the most important parts are to address. Don't dwell on the previous question and what you could have said. It is too late! However, if you worry about it and can't get it out of your head, then make a quick note to return to it later and instead concentrate on the question being put. You can even alert the panel by asking, 'Is it OK that I add something further on the last question at the end if there is enough time?'

Be wary about pressure questions or tests designed to stress or anger you. They may be judging how you respond under pressure or intimidation. Keep calm no matter what is said.

Do not speak poorly of past employers as the panel would not want to employ somebody who may later potentially damage their reputation also. You may also be seen as overcritical or a complainer!

Have some questions prepared that are not already answered in any literature you have been given! It can be annoying to waste valuable time. In a later chapter, see samples of questions you can ask.

Revealing Your Aspirations

You may be asked about your career goals—e.g. 'Where would you like to be in five years?', 'What have you done to achieve any current goals?', or 'Where do you hope this job will take you?' The interviewer is looking for motivation, initiative, whether your aspirations are realistic, and whether you intend to stay. Prepare a one-minute answer to this question before the interview.

Tip: As stated elsewhere, do not say that you will have left or started your own business or expect to be the boss! Refer to some guidelines on answering these questions in the 'Thirty-Five Common Interview Questions and Their Answers' section that follows.

What Interests Are Safe to Disclose?

Outside interests and hobbies may be discussed, and you may not realise their value to the work at the time. This may be with the intent to discover your motivations and commitment. It may also indicate your level of involvement and participation in committees or organisational activities which may help improve skills required in the role. There may be hobbies that directly relate to the job (e.g. photography for somebody in marketing and advertising).

However, if you disclose too many outside interests, it may make the employer nervous that your energy and time will be used elsewhere. Similarly, try not to sound too obsessed about any particular interest. Keep this period of discussion brief.

If asked about TV-watching habits, try not to sound like a couch potato, but have good reasons for being selective on what you watch (e.g. you like watching educational and motivational shows but also watch some for relaxation as a balance to any of your physically active recreations).

Try to discover and talk (briefly) about the interviewer's interests or at least pick up on them during the conversation. At times, interests can be identified by observing objects around the office. Preferably, they are work-related, and by sharing some common experiences, you can develop a better rapport and relationship. This strategy is obviously easier and more appropriate when you have a single interviewer rather than a panel.

Questions that Reveal the Desired Response

Some questions will indicate what the interviewer is looking for (e.g. a school teacher may be asked whether they took part in any extracurricular activities). This says that the interviewer believes this to be important. Another example would be 'This job requires a motivated self-starter, are you able to perform like that?' Clearly, the desired response is that you would agree! Back this up with an example of when you worked without the need for supervision.

Another example may be 'How do you feel about occasionally working overtime?' The interviewer is revealing that this is important, and thus you shouldn't answer with 'I must leave on time every day due to other commitments'. This shows inflexibility, but if it was actually an issue for you and real commitments prevent it, then you can be honest and hope you are thus not rejected. Consider whether this job is actually not what you wanted after clarifying the employer's expectations.

Thirty-Five Common Interview Questions and Their Answers

The following present some of the commonly asked questions and openers at interviews. It is therefore good practice to consider your possible answers, and as an aid, there are some key points presented. Some variations to each question are also presented alongside or via a word within brackets. However, it is best to not learn these as rote answers but to use your own words where possible as it will sound more convincing and less like it is coming from somebody else. As all interviews are different, one cannot guarantee that any of the following questions will be included.

1) 'Tell me about yourself' or 'Can you introduce yourself to me?' or 'How would a good friend or colleague describe you?'

   Prepare a brief statement on your education and work history and what positive attributes you bring to the job (e.g. need to succeed, attention to detail, people person). Gain clues on what to talk about from the wording in the advert. Avoid irrelevant background as much as possible, though hobbies or sports that may add some positive attributes could be included. However, don't start telling your favourite sporting stories. Have a list of positive attributes ready that may come from colleagues or friends but be careful not to overstate these as some claims could be verified by referee checks later. You could also narrow down the answer by asking the interviewer if there is any particular aspect in your background they want to focus on.

2) 'What do you enjoy doing on the weekends or for leisure time?'

   Watch out for disclosing any highly physical, risk activities, and try to focus on those that provide fitness or other skills that can relate to the job. If you do competitive sports that involve travel, then consider its possible impact on your future work. The fact that you may be involved in relaxing activities on weekends after a physically heavy or intellectually challenging weekday job can be seen as an important part of stress reduction. Obviously, avoid revealing that you may drink a lot down the bar! Voluntary work or helping others in another capacity (e.g. team sports roles) may bring out other positive attributes to the interviewer.

3) 'Have you ever done this kind of work before?'

   If not, never say no, but instead focus on the skills that can be translated to this job. This is your chance to talk about the relevance of your past experience. Try to mention all aspects of previous job tasks and duties that are the same or are related to this one. Try to add some key achievements or awards/acknowledgments gained for your work. You want to sound confident about your abilities and potential to learn new skills. Examples of how quick you are to learn may also help here.

4) 'How long have you been looking for a job?' or 'Why haven't you found another job yet?'

   Your answer may focus on waiting for the right job to match your skills and goals and thus being appropriately selective. If you had other offers that didn't meet your needs, then disclose this also. The basic response is that you have found that this job appears to offer the challenges you are seeking and will utilise the skills you have developed.

5) 'Why have you changed jobs so frequently?'

   Firstly, try to avoid listing so many jobs in your résumé so that this is less noticeable. Try a functional-style résumé (CV). However, it may be that you were contracted for projects only or that there were family reasons for having to move. The point is that sometimes it can be easily explained. You may say that some of the previous workplaces did not allow you to develop and utilise your skills, and thus you continued searching for that right culture.

However, you might also consider saying that you were unsure of your directions initially and had to experience different workplaces and roles before now deciding on your direction. Now that you are sure, you are prepared to stay and apply your talents to the job. You may have found the drive to career progression and hope to remain and prove your value in such a business where success is recognised by promotions. You don't want to say you were easily bored by previous jobs and didn't get on with the people there!

You may have done a lot of temp work, and maybe you can sell the fact that you are highly sought for such positions due to your easily transferrable skills and ability to learn quickly. Focus on the positive aspects of having done temp work (e.g. varied skills acquired).

6) 'What do you think is needed to be successful in this job?' or 'Why do you think you will be successful?'

   Look for clues in the job description or advert prior to the interview. Focus on such attributes as competence, willingness to learn, quickness to learn, being able to enjoy working with others, attitude, drive to succeed, being open to instruction, being able to apply your skills to the best of your ability, being a good team player, etc. Basically, you hold the right skills, experience, and attitude to succeed.

7) 'Why do you want this job?' or 'Why do you wish to work here?' or 'Why do you want to work for us?'

   This question tests the motivation behind your job application. You may be able to drop some facts found about them from your pre-interview research and show how this makes them a desirable place to work. Include compliments about their culture, their success, and how this is a place you would thrive under and thus bring out your best work. However, remember this is more about what you can give them than what you want! For example, you believe you can make a positive contribution.

Focus on having a good match for skills, natural progression of your skills, better utilisation of your skills than the last job, career progression, etc. Don't make it just about the pay or needing money! Avoid generic statements of what you like unless you can expand on them with examples (e.g. instead of saying something such as 'I like working with people', add the reasons why). Don't offer complaints about current work being the reason for your application.

8) 'Why should we hire you instead of someone else [an insider]?'

Don't see this as a personal challenge and get defensive. Ask them to clarify what kind of person they are seeking. Provide a quick summary list of your major skills, education, and experience relevant to the job. Your aim is to convince them that you can add value or meet their expectations! Don't present yourself as being arrogant though! You can bring new skills and strengths to their team. Relate it to what their business needs as identified through your research or their information at the interview.

Finish with a statement of your desire to achieve and your strong work ethic. Check with them if there was anything else they were looking for or if your response covered what was needed. Address any shortfall identified before moving on to the next question. On the issue of insiders, sometimes new blood is sought out as new people to the business can bring different experiences and ideas which could provide benefits.

9) 'What can you offer us by working here?'

Have a summary prepared prior to the interview of your relevant experience, skills, successes, and attributes which establish how you fit in with their team. Refer also to the answers to questions 7 and 8 above for more ideas.

10) 'I'm not sure you are suitable for the job. Wouldn't you be better off at . . . ?'

    Don't be put off by this as it is just another way of asking why you want to work there and why they should choose you. It is a test of your commitment to this job and a form of stress question also. Don't get defensive, and focus your answer as you would on the previous few examples.

11) 'What do you think about relocation [fly-in-fly-out work]?'

    This is something you should have considered prior to the application, and so be prepared to negotiate conditions if offered the job. It would be helpful to state that you have discussed this with your partner (spouse) and have reached agreement that it can be accommodated. You should emphasise how quickly adaptable you are to changed conditions and that there are no particular ties to remaining in your current residence.

12) 'How would you get started on the job?' or 'What would you do if you were hired for this job?'

    Earlier in this book, there were guidelines on preparing a ninety-day action plan that could also be appropriate to relate here. You would aim to learn all relevant policies and procedures as soon as possible, identify work expectations, and meet all key personnel. You may also look for ways to make a positive contribution to their success.

13) 'Why did you [do you want to] leave your last [current] job?'

    Make it a positive move, such as career progression, aligning yourself with their business with its size and image, greater opportunities to utilise your particular skills, achieve more, and take on greater responsibility. Hence, you are thus seeking a better fit for your skills or the opportunity to take your skills to the next level. Do not talk of negative issues (complaints)—being sacked, that you didn't like the last boss/supervisor, or didn't like how they did things there, etc. In some cases, there are more basic reasons, such as excessive commute time or uncertain business survival in difficult economic times.

14) 'Have you ever been fired or asked to resign? Why?'

If you lie, you run the risk of being found out through reference checks with a former employer. However, your answer may vary depending on whether it was about you directly or a general downsizing in the company. The latter is more understandable as you may have been employed for a lesser time than others. If it was about personal differences, skills deficit, or an unfortunate event, then try to turn it into a positive, and don't get too emotional (bitter, angry) or defensive talking about it. Say something along the lines that you have had time to reflect and learn from the situation and believe it would not happen again as you have since gained skills, practice, confidence, etc. in that area. There may have been additional ways you improved yourself (e.g. personal-development classes). You could say that your being fired was justified (taking responsibility) due to personal issues you were going through at that time but are now resolved.

15) 'What do [did] you find stimulating about your current [last] job?'

Focus on goals attained and maybe the great team you worked with. You may enjoy being able to use your initiative to solve problems and make improvements in the workplace. Furthermore, you have found it motivating to have your ideas acknowledged and respected. You find it rewarding in being able to make a difference in the workplace or to the success of the business. Be prepared to spell out how you made that difference. Your response may also focus on the nature of the work itself or that you thrive on challenges that help you develop your skills. Your response may also include the varied people you worked with and maybe something about a fast-paced or a dynamic environment with learning opportunities.

16) 'What do [did] you dislike most at your current [previous] work?'

    Be careful here! Avoid spelling out situations you will likely face again in this workplace. Thus, consider disclosing an issue from a previous workplace that is unlikely to happen in this one, and maybe turn this into a positive about why you would like it here better (e.g. this new business may offer better professional development training, excellent customer service, promotional opportunities, better management policies, more effective budget management, recognised leadership).

17) 'What appeals to you least about this job?'

    Again, be careful here! Try to consider a pre-interview point after considering the job description, and make it a small unimportant part of the job. Reassure the interviewer that you consider all aspects of the job important and that you will be equally diligent in this aspect of least interest to you. All jobs carry something like this, but you just get on with it without complaint. You may also find ways to minimise the problem or at least keep it under control (e.g. emails, unnecessary disruptions, paperwork). Be careful about disclosing factors such as travel or long hours as that may indicate you will only stay until something better comes along!

18) 'Tell me a little more about what you did in your last [on a previous] job.'

    Try to point out all duties and skills that most closely align with this new job. You should have considered the job description or duty statement as part of your preparation.

19) 'What kind of salary do you need? Do you know the going rate?'

    Refer to the section on salary questions in the next chapter for strategies in dealing with this question and area of negotiation.

20) 'What do you look [are you looking] for in a job [your next job]?'

Don't focus on what you want personally (e.g. pay and hours). Focus on the opportunity to use the special skills you have, to be able to make a positive contribution, and to be recognised for such, including potential career advancement. You can claim to value the satisfaction that accompanies a job that is well done. Use examples of past achievements that you would like to build on in the next job. Consider also saying that you enjoy working in a productive team.

21) 'How will you contribute [add value] to our company's success?'

Again, consider preparing a spiel on this prior to the interview, and include your best attributes and background that fit this job. You may provide examples of how you started or led initiatives in the past to show you can be an asset. Tell of any actions that resulted in time savings or cost reductions for the business. Have confidence and sell yourself! You may need to enquire about what priorities they see you working on and then respond on how you can use your talents in that area. By asking this question, you may get them picturing you in the job and thus assisting with your favourable selection.

22) 'What will you do to make a difference?'

Discuss how you would use your skills and knowledge to meet all expectations as well as contribute ideas to improve efficiency whenever identified. Discuss achievements in the past that led to savings in time through more efficient processes, reduced costs, your expertise applied to training others, etc. For private-sector jobs, focus on your impact on important aspects of the business, such as sales, profits, customers. You may also add about being an effective team player, being reliable, and being goal-oriented. You may also be a fast and productive worker.

23) 'How is your health?'

Be honest, but don't give up too many negatives if they do not seem relevant. If you have a good, low sick-leave record, then say so. You may state that 'I am fit for this job, and this will be verified by any health screening required'. If you engage in a sport or other keep-fit activities, then say so to emphasise your current fitness. Many job offers are subject to an approved pre-employment medical.

24) 'When are you available to start work?' or 'If we offered you the job, would you take it?'

The answer should be 'As soon as required, but after giving adequate or the required notice to my current employer'. Your pre-interview preparation should include consideration of a probable start date so you look confident when asked rather than unprepared, uncertain, and flustered by the question.

You may test the waters with respect to any vacation time desired before starting, but be prepared to compromise or drop this if you really want the job and a quick start is needed. The question of whether you would take the job has to be an affirmative answer, but you may qualify it with something like 'Yes, I am very interested from what I have found thus far in my pre-interview research and here at the interview.'

25) 'How were you able to attend this interview today?'

Be careful of being trapped into disclosing dishonesty if currently employed and your boss does not know of your attending this interview—especially in paid work time! If you are being dishonest with the time taken from your current employ, then of course you can do it again to this new employer! Either your boss knows you are attending and condones it or you should be utilising accrued leave. (Don't say you took a sickie!). Of course, if you are between jobs or maybe you are off shift that day, then this is not an issue.

26) 'What are your long-term goals?' or 'Where do you want to be in five years?' or 'Can you see yourself still working here in ten years?' or 'How long do you intend to stay with the company?'

These are all related questions, and you may consider opening with a question back identifying what opportunities there are in the business. Consider their answer to guide you in your prepared response. You may reply that you will stay as long as you are achieving and making a positive contribution. Focus on career progression, giving back to the business through mentoring newer employees, becoming more competent and being recognised for it, etc. Do not say you intend to retire, start your own business, or expect to be the boss!

27) 'What do you know about our company/organisation?'

Have a prepared brief summary to impress them on your research. Do not bring up any negatives. Do not say you know very little or nothing! You can use some flattery if appropriate, but don't overdo it.

28) 'What sort of business do you want to work for, and why?'

Your research should have informed you about what the company offers and what they are like to work for. Hence, use that information to inform your reply. Besides saying something positive about the industry or the company's reputation, you may also allude to potential opportunities for advancement and their recognition of successful employees. In other words, you like to work for a company that values achievement. It could also be a business that offers good career pathways which you will find stimulating and enable you to develop new skills.

29) 'Do you get along well with people?'

Avoid saying anything that indicates poor teamwork, not being able to follow instructions, being a loner, or having interpersonal conflicts. Also avoid alluding to the fact that you don't get along with certain types of people or those you find annoying for whatever reason. Focus more on the positive contribution that working with others makes in job satisfaction, teamwork, and learning from different points of view. You may consider adding that you are open to other people's views, are approachable, and respect cultural differences. You find it stimulating to work with a variety of people.

30) 'What are your strengths and weaknesses?' or 'What is your greatest weakness?'

You should have prepared for this question prior to the interview and easily tell of strengths relevant to the job. Try to back up strengths with objective accomplishments, such as increased sales, presented efficiencies or cost savings, projects running to time and budget, and tasks that demonstrated organisational ability. Find examples relevant to your occupation. On the subject of weaknesses, only refer to a limited weakness. Don't respond by saying that you do not have any weaknesses as you will present yourself as being arrogant. However, don't mention any weaknesses that are difficult to overcome or may be replicated in this new job.

You need to give something, but make it something you have already recognised and corrected. You will then get a positive mark rather than a negative. You may consider using an example of a virtue that you may give as a weakness (e.g. the time it takes paying attention to detail or 'I find it hard working with people who do not carry a full load'). If the panel recognises this tactic, then be prepared with another example. The weakness should be phrased more as an area for improvement that you have already recognised and done something to correct. Alternatively, if the weakness is about experience with a particular task (or software), report on what you have done that is related and what a quick learner you were. Have more than one example available in case they ask for more!

31) 'What is your greatest failure?'

Be careful here to choose an example that is not critical to your future employment. Maybe something along the lines of not being clear enough in directions given in delegation but that now you have learned from this and you give clearer instructions—and check that they have been interpreted correctly! As with the weaknesses question, tell of how you learned from that failure and now have taken measures to ensure it will not be repeated. This is necessary to dampen any concerns about repeated behaviours/ failures. You may also consider a self-imposed failure, such as not having the self-confidence to go for career advancement earlier in your career. You have now recognised that your skills deserve to be acknowledged through promotion.

32) 'What has been your biggest challenge?'

Carefully consider this one prior to the interview, and be aware that they may be evaluating what you actually find challenging. For example, it should not be about working with other people! Keep it to a non-critical area of work and try to make it a positive characteristic (e.g. being a perfectionist or desire to work beyond normal hours). Alternatively, use an event/project that you were tasked with organising and how it required all your talents to achieve that really positive result. Choose an example that had a good result and demonstrated your organisational and problem-solving skills. The challenge may relate to a tight deadline or having inadequate resources to complete a task efficiently and how you overcame the adversity.

33) 'What have been your most significant work achievements [biggest accomplishments] to date?'

Prepare a list prior to the interview and select examples with the most relevance to this particular job, and the more recent, the better. Consider key projects performed and met on time. Consider complex tasks learned with now-recognised expertise. Consider work with teams, culture-change initiatives, meeting objective business targets, or exceeding them. If your accomplishment was more as part of a team, then build upon your active participation in the team. You could conclude that you expect to aim for even higher benchmarks in the future in that you are still growing in experience and skills. At times, there may also be a great non-work team achievement you can explain. Try to explain what made it such an achievement so that the interviewer fully understands what you had to overcome.

34) 'Describe your best and worst boss [or job] and explain why' or 'Describe the greatest weakness of a former boss'

Be as positive as you can and downplay the bad by not being overly critical. Consider discussing possible worst aspects, such as issues like lack of support for staff or condoned inefficiencies of practice. Even if there were many things to complain about, it would not be wise to disclose them now. Don't be seen as a complainer! Similar to the question about your own greatest weakness, try to put a positive spin on any perceived shortcomings (e.g. the former boss enjoyed such a good relationship with their staff that they sometimes found it difficult making hard decisions).

35) 'How do you handle criticism?'

You basically have to say that you accept constructive criticism as that is a way of learning and making improvements to your skills. If they then ask about what seems unreasonable criticism, say that you will not act defensively but take time to reflect on what has been said. If you still believe the criticism is unfounded, you would ask for a discussion to understand the other's point of view and to raise your points without being argumentative. Aim for a better understanding of expectations.

Questions on Pay (Salary)

As a minimum for preparation, you must know what your current salary is, including any fringe benefits. If you are unsure, then check with your current Human Resources or payroll staff. At times, people may be wary of asking within their current employ as they do not want to disclose seeking jobs elsewhere. Hence, without disclosing your real reasons, you could say it is about financial planning, considering a loan, preparing a family budget, etc.

Take great care with your answer if the interviewer asks you what you expect to be paid if employed. If you go too high, you may price yourself out of the job at this stage. If too low, you will appear to undervalue yourself, which may lead them to the same opinion. Worse still, they may employ you at this low-wage level instead of what they may have previously been prepared to pay.

It is thus essential to research salaries prior to the interview so you know the ballpark or range of pays for that kind of job. Responding with a realistic range, perhaps guided by the job advert, is better than a set figure. However, go to the interview with a bottom line in mind. Take account of the realistic differences between what a large business versus small business may be able to afford. If they are large with a significant turnover, then higher salaries may be more affordable.

You may like to send the question back by asking, 'What salary range is on offer?' or 'What is the salary range for similar jobs here?' or 'My understanding is that the salary range for jobs such as this will range from *x* to *y* dollars, depending on skills and experience'. Another possible answer is 'I trust you to pay somebody in this position a fair salary'. Alternatively, you could reply that 'As I like the job you are offering, I will accept a reasonable offer'. They then may move on, and you can negotiate the actual level once they offer you the job. However, if you believe you are worth a certain value, then confidently assert your reasons.

Tip: you may consider doing further reading on how to negotiate pay to gain greater skills if you still lack confidence.

The first person to answer the pay question in a negotiation is considered the loser. You are in a better position to negotiate once you know they want to employ you. Of course in some posts, such as in the public sector, there may be state or national industrial awards with set, non-negotiable conditions. You can always check with the Personnel or Human Resources Department as to whether this applies.

Also, there may be other (fringe) benefits to consider other than just the base pay, so do not be too quick to accept initial offers. Take a list of your current benefits with you to refer to if needed. Salary packaging may be available, so look to the non-pay benefits when negotiating (e.g. parking, travel, education support, and vehicle). Depending on your industry and occupation, you may like to know about leave provisions, stock options, bonuses, pay in lieu of vacations, common fringe benefits, or benefits such as medical or dental plans also (generally outside Australia). However, it is not recommended to ask all these at the interview, or it will look like you are more interested in conditions like time off than the job! Remember to hold off on much of this negotiation until actually offered the job.

Another factor to enquire about is pension plans or superannuation. The latter is now legislated in Australia to be paid at a minimum amount once certain conditions of employment or minimum wage levels are met. Check on what is applicable in your country.

Tip: At times, a lower base pay may be more than compensated by other benefits. You will need to set a value on these in making your decision on what salary to accept.

If you want to bargain a little more, you may say that you are being interviewed for posts paying *x* dollars and that you would not be happy accepting less. You may also mention your research findings into industry pay levels. In any event, do not be too aggressive on this and turn the potential new employer against you. Remain polite and interested and not confrontational! They are also not usually interested in your personal financial problems dictating how much you need as it is about the job and your value to them.

If you are asked to reveal what you are being paid currently, then firstly keep in mind that they may be able to verify whatever you claim through the current employer. Should the other job pay less, then it is your tactic to point out why the other job is sufficiently different to justify a higher salary for this one.

Questions that Should Not Be Asked by the Interviewer

It may be unlawful to ask questions which may be considered irrelevant to successfully performing the job. If a question is discriminatory, then an offence may be committed (e.g. Equal Employment Opportunity Act in Australia). Some companies or organisations achieve dispensations to discriminate on certain factors (e.g. gender) if they can demonstrate it is necessary for the job or culture.

The question may be asked out of ignorance or arrogance. At times, it may be asked just to see how you would react or respond to such pressure, so maintain your self-control!

You may choose to risk offending the interviewer by asking how this relates to the job or maybe politely saying that you find the question inappropriate. In some positions, what may seem discriminatory may be a valid attribute to seek. It may be best to respond indirectly by just reassuring the interviewer that you can manage the needs of the job. You may say that whatever your situation is, the job always comes first and that you take your responsibilities very seriously.

You cannot claim discrimination on grounds of merit where you believe you were better qualified for the job than the successful candidate. However, if you believed that you were discriminated against on the grounds outlined under the relevant act, then you may choose to pursue a complaint later.

You may research local equal-opportunity acts or other antidiscrimination acts for further details on what should not be asked and what actions you can take if experiencing such discrimination. There may also be applicable disability acts offering additional protections if you have a disability.

Some potentially discriminatory questions could be:

- Are you married? Are you single/divorced/separated?
- Do you have children or plan to have any?
- What will you do with the children while you are at work?
- What will you do if the children get sick?
- What is your religion?
- Do you have a disability? (May prevent work of some kinds but may be tested by medical or job skills test.)
- Whom do you follow in politics? Which party did you vote for?
- How old are you? (NB: don't include date of birth in your CV.)
- Aren't you too old for this work?
- Other areas considered potentially discriminatory include questions on race (or ethnic origins), your parents, and sexual orientation.

Checklist on How to Fail at an Interview!

The following statements outline succinctly what you would avoid if you planned to succeed in a job interview:

- Be totally unprepared, having done no research.
- Arrive late without good reason.
- Do not understand the job you have applied for.
- Simply do not have the skills or knowledge they are looking for.
- Look and dress inappropriately for an interview.
- Chew gum, belch, pass wind, fidget too much, look grumpy, etc.
- Mumble, swear, and frequently use slang words.
- Talk excessively and ramble about irrelevant information.
- Do not look the interviewer in the eye.
- Be overly critical of others in your replies.
- Be evasive and make excuses for an unfavourable work history.
- Be overly critical of their business and say what you would do to fix it.
- Argue with the panel.
- When asking your questions, focus a lot on sick leave and holidays.
- Respond to questions by just shrugging.
- If asked about past problems or weaknesses, say none.
- Apply restrictions on the job like 'I won't be wearing any uniform!'
- Be overly familiar or overly personal with panel members.
- Give the impression you know it all and there is nothing more to learn.

- Be overly boastful and also drop names to imply you should be given the job.
- Interrupt the interviewer on more than one occasion.
- Don't show any interest in the process by looking bored and distracted.
- Roll your eyes at their questions.
- Make rude comments about not seeing the point of their questions.
- Put your foot in your mouth by being insensitive and politically incorrect.
- Keep looking at your watch as if you have somewhere better to be.
- Take phone calls during the interview.
- Give the impression you don't care if you get the job.
- Have no questions when invited to ask.
- Have no idea when they ask when you could start.
- Lie and overembellish (in the CV also).
- Ask if they require a drug test!

Dealing with the Bad Interviewer

At times, you will face a poor interviewer who may be obviously biased, sexist, or rude, and you may choose to ignore this and do your best. Be cautious that this is not just an act designed to test you and your tolerance to stress, emotional control, etc. They may also be testing your determination to win the job.

At times, you may decide that you do not want to work for this person or business. You may then consider excusing yourself from the interview and withdrawing your application. Don't storm out, but take charge by assertively telling them how you have been treated and that you do not want to work for such a company that condones such practices. A complaint to the business may be useful so that if it is an employee (not the boss) who has conducted the interview, then corrective measures may be taken. This person needs remedial action, and the feedback may not have been previously received. This may benefit others in the future from experiencing the same bad experience.

If the interviewer looks like they will be spending all your interview time talking about themselves or the business, then do find ways to carefully interject by demonstrating knowledge you have about the subject being discussed. Remember, this may be your only chance to influence the decision, and you will not be able to make a proper impression if the other party does all the talking!

A poor interviewer will often ask questions that just need a yes or no answer when by rewording the question they can get a more detailed answer. When this happens, try not to say yes or no (unless appropriate to that question) but expand with more information that may showcase your talents, experience, etc.

If the interviewer is poorly prepared and hesitates on what questions to ask, then try to take charge and lead the discussion into areas where you want to impress them. This may be your one chance to win that job. Be careful though that they do not think they are being interrogated. Try to maintain the image that they are in charge of the process (e.g. 'Would you like me to discuss my experience in . . . ?' gives them the power to choose or redirect).

Another example of a poor interviewer is one who allows interruptions. Use any such time to reflect on how things are going and what else you should emphasise. Remind the interviewer of where you were up to when recommencing (e.g. 'We were just discussing . . .'). Therefore, use whatever time you gain effectively and try not to get annoyed.

An interviewer may seem hostile and aggressive, but try not to respond in kind. Try to keep calm and assume it is only a test of your resolve and personal control under pressure.

At the end of the day, we can all have an off day, so be patient, use tact, and remain composed through the interview, which will be appreciated by the interviewer.

The Interview Close

Expectations and Actions at the Close

You may be asked some closing questions or be invited to ask your own or perhaps be given the opportunity to add anything further in support of your application. This may be followed by information on the next step, such as when a decision may be made or in some cases consideration of a second interview. In some processes, there may also be an additional step of some take-home assignment to complete. Consider the possibilities in professions such as photography, journalism, advertising, and marketing.

You will usually be told if any appeal provisions are applicable (usually through public service). Finally, you will then be thanked and shown out.

If you think you answered some questions poorly, do not apologise as it indicates a lack of confidence in yourself. Perhaps you may instead state that 'Upon reflection, I would like to add . . . to the question on . . .'. Remember that few people are perfect at the interview, and you are being compared with others who equally may have presented less-than-complete answers. Very few people enjoy an interview, and many go away with negative self-reflection on what they should have said or what they said poorly. The purpose of this book is indeed to reduce that from occurring due to good preparation and winning strategies.

There are actions you can take after the interview to increase your chances or to gain valuable feedback on your performance. Please refer to the next chapter for more on these strategies.

It is essential that you use this time effectively as the last impressions can be as important as the first.

Common Closing Questions by the Interviewer

- 'What kind of salary do you need?'

  For possible ways of dealing with this question, including responding with a range, refer to the earlier section on handling questions about pay.

- 'When are you available to start work?'

  Make it reasonable after taking account of any periods of notice required to any current employer. You may also reply with 'When do you need me to start?' Then consider whether you want to take a short vacation between jobs before nominating the date. Refer also to the commonly asked questions section, under number 24.

- 'Is there anything else you would like to say in support of your application?'

  Have your prepared spiel ready which reinforces both your commitment to the job and that you possess what they are looking for.

- 'Do you have any concerns about the job?'

  Save these for after being offered the job rather than sew doubts now!

Questions You Could Ask

Often the discussion at the interview and the job description details will let you know the answers to most of your questions. However, it is best to ask at least one smart question to reinforce your enthusiasm in working there. Don't give the impression that you are without a question. Make your questions intelligent ones. Consider writing down some important questions in case you forget them on the day. However, you probably do not want to take up too much time as other people may be scheduled to be interviewed after you. Do not look to be interrogating the interviewer but ask questions politely (e.g. consider the difference between 'Tell me about your policy on *x*' and 'May I ask about your policy on *x*?')

Don't ask a question you have already been given the answer to earlier in the interview—pay attention! Similarly, do not waste their time by asking questions about things you should already know or were answered in the job application package. Asking questions that are clearly answered by the employer in their job application material, advert, or website may indicate a failure on your part to research the job. Do not ask questions which hold no interest to you as the interviewer can usually tell and then of course think you are just wasting their time!

You may ask about instigating an improvement at their workplace and ask how they would feel about that. (Don't offend them first with your overly critical observation!)

Never ask if you have got the job as it may be seen as rude. Do not ask the interviewer how you went as it may show lack of confidence and will trigger only a polite response. Consider phrasing the question in a different way to demonstrate greater confidence and increase the likelihood of a more helpful response. For example, begin with a positive summary of your skills as they relate to any selection criteria and then move on to your question. 'If I were not selected for this job, what would the reasons be?' Alternatively, ask, 'Did I answer all the questions to your satisfaction, or are there any concerns or reservations that I may address before leaving?' You may be asked why you asked (checking your self-confidence), so have a good reply ready. You could say, 'It is because I want to ensure that I fit in with your requirements.'

If some reservations are raised, then respond to them with examples to overcome their fears. Do this at the end when other questions have been dealt with.

Avoid questions that give negative impressions of where your priorities lie. For example, about salary (as mentioned previously), about how much leave you can take, about workers compensation, and lunch breaks. Remember that these can be dealt with once the job has been offered.

Avoid asking questions that show you are hesitant about being employed there (e.g. the chance of redundancy or business failure). Similarly, avoid questions that show you have certain reservations, such as 'Would I have to work with . . . ?'
If you remain uncertain about the job or boss, then consider asking them about the people working for the company, past projects, directions of the business, etc. It may help you gain a better impression of what they may be like to work for and whether the company is moving in a positive and interesting direction.

Whether you ask one or more questions will be determined by the time available and what remains unanswered. At times, the interview questions and discussion will disclose problem areas in the business. If you hear such problems mentioned, you can ask whether there will be any implications for the job.

The following list will provide some ideas on what may be relevant questions under different circumstances or occupations. Consider what you need the answer to or any other issues you want clarified. Again, be aware of how much time is available to you and what has been answered elsewhere.

Other Questions You Might Select From

- What would be my main tasks in the first two to three months?
- What would you expect me to achieve in the first six months?
- Would I be working with a small or large team?

(Any of these first three will force the interviewer to picture you in the job and reinforce your choice as a candidate.)

- Are there opportunities for advancement?
- What would be the best and worst aspects of this job?
- What is the typical career progression?
- Is there a typical time frame for promotion?
- What are the skills most needed to get ahead in this company?
- Is there a staff induction/orientation programme? Other training programmes?
- What is a typical day like in the job?
- What do you consider as priorities to somebody starting out?
- Can you describe an ideal employee?
- Will I be working on my own? Can you tell me about the team I will be working with? (This should be obvious for most jobs.)
- Why is the position open? (New post, resignation, termination, etc.)
- When should I expect to hear back from you? (Only a priority question if you are waiting on another offer.)
- What is the next step in the hiring process?
- What are the hours of work?
- Are there any flexible working arrangements, like flexitime? (Be prepared to back up why you asked.)
- Is there any overtime to be done? Any weekend work?
- If a uniform or protective clothing is required, is it provided by the employer?
- Where is the job located, and how much business travel is required?
- How often are employees relocated or transferred?
- What level of responsibility do you expect me to take in this position?
- Can you describe your performance management process?
- Are there opportunities or support for continuing education?
- How do you see this organisation (business) growing (expanding) in the future?
- How important is this position to the organisation?
- Are there any significant changes planned for this area?
- What do you like most about working for this organisation?
- How does this organisation treat its employees?

When Invited to Make a Final Statement

The interviewer may ask something like 'Would you like to say something in support of your application?' or 'Can you summarise why we should choose you?' or 'Is there anything we haven't covered?' There are a number of options available to you at this point. Refer to the guidelines provided under question 8 in the common interview questions section for some advice.

Your response could be to say how much you have enjoyed the interview and to reaffirm how much you want the job. You may even add a compliment about their company, reiterating why you chose to apply to them.

Be prepared to summarise why you want the job and why they should hire you. This may be your one and only chance to impress. In expressing why you want the job, do not just say it's for the money, because you just need a job, because it is close to home, etc. Remember, the employer is looking for somebody who will stay in the job and who wants it for the right reasons. They have invested time and money in the selection process and will then spend time and money in your orientation, job skills training, etc. Hence, they do not want it wasted on somebody that leaves as soon as possible. Some degree of loyalty is expected. Emphasise that you have the abilities and skills to make a good fit and that they offer opportunities to best utilise those skills.

Take-Home Assignments

Some positions and selection processes may include a task to complete after the interview. Ensure you understand what is required, when it should be submitted, how it should be presented, and where to deliver it once completed (e.g. a sample marketing plan, photographic assignment, graphic designs, and education delivery plan). Obviously, this will apply only to particular industries and occupations.

Farewells

Straighten up your clothes when standing up and gather any items brought to the interview. When leaving the interview room, thank each interviewer in turn with a handshake and address them by their right names to impress. Ask for business cards if not previously offered. Close the door behind you quietly. If you are escorted down to the reception or exit, then do not let your guard down, but continue with proper decorum.

Ask when a decision will be made as this may assist with your post-interview strategies outlined in the next chapter. You may also ask for preferred contact details in case you have any follow-up questions.

Section 4

Post-Interview Strategies

Post-Interview Process and Strategies

What the Interviewers Will Be Doing

If the process is structured and well organised, the interview panel will assess you against all requirements for the job. If unstructured with no particular accountability for the process, a decision may be made on gut feeling and other personal factors. There is little you can do about that except utilise the interview strategies outlined in this book to make a favourable impression.

The panel may use a numerical rating scale when judging your answers and performance. Sometimes criteria that they consider more important to the job are weighted, so the score counts for more. They can use these scores to rank applicants and offer jobs in order of ranking. You may be placed into a pool for future selection as jobs occur.

Scoring may be completed by panel members, either individually or in collaboration with a final mark agreed upon. There may be a standardised scoring index used by the organisation, or they may apply their own rules (e.g. a mark out of ten for each standard question). A standardised index mark per question or criterion may be something like this:

4 = exceptional or significantly above average
3 = well above average
2 = satisfactory/average level
1 = meets criteria at a minimum level and needs development
0 = doesn't meet criteria.

You can see that it is still a somewhat subjective process. Marks may be given for each good point in your answer to particular questions, then added and possibly scaled back into a category like the above.

The panel will usually evaluate factors such as experience, qualifications, background, and education. They may also evaluate more-subjective factors, such as enthusiasm, personality, and the right fit (i.e. whether they believe you will fit in with others in their workplace). This area may not be openly assessed but always plays a role in decisions whether they are objective or otherwise.

Next, they may seek written or verbal reports from one or more referees. This can be in the nature of a standard assessment against all criteria or other standard details with more-general questions, such as 'Would that person employ you again?' At times, the interviewers want to delve or probe more into specific criteria, maybe where they hold reservations or have to be completely confident of those abilities. It is important that you have supportive referees and they should be prepared to be contacted.

Tip: If you had to prepare a written statement addressing the selection criteria as part of the process, then it is recommended that you provide a copy to your referees also. They do not always know about certain aspects of your background skills and experience, so this will help them respond when asked.

If your referees receive a request to complete a referee report form, either in writing or online, then request a prompt response from them as the selection process cannot conclude until such reports have been received by the panel.

Once a decision is made, the employer will contact the first choice to confirm they will accept the job and, once accepted, will usually notify the other applicants. Some employers will not contact unsuccessful applicants and will tell you that unless you hear from them (in a set time) that you have missed out, there will be no correspondence. Sometimes offers are made subject to an appeal period.—that is, unsuccessful applicants are invited to appeal within a set time if they think that the process went against general equal-opportunity standards (e.g. public-service standards for government employees).

If you haven't heard in a reasonable time (e.g. a week), then this could indicate that the first choice is still taking time to respond or that the employer has not made their decision or that nobody went well and they are considering re-advertising. It may also be a delay caused by seeking referee reports or perhaps they are still interviewing further applicants. Feel free to contact the employer again to see what is happening unless of course they expressly told you not to!

At other times, no news does not equate with bad news. At times, there is no immediate job available and the employer (or agency) is developing a list or pool of suitable candidates for the future. A job pool may be progressively used over time to select candidates for future vacancies. At times, the method will be based on the highest scorers or rank, and at other times, candidates may be selected on their attributes or strengths that are required by the company at that time.

Importance of the Thank-You Correspondence

Consider sending a thank-you letter or email that can also reinforce any key points from the interview or includes important points you missed at the interview. It must be received very quickly after the interview (less than twenty-four hours preferably) and prior to a decision being finalised. It must be addressed to the main interviewer; ensure the name is spelt correctly. Watch your spelling and grammar so they don't get a bad impression at this point. It should generally be not more than one page in length, plus any additional documents mentioned below.

Some selection processes take a while to conclude due to:

- people being interviewed on several days or weeks
- the panel taking time to reconvene after the interviews to make a decision
- the time taken in following up on referee reports
- the possibility of a second interview
- time off by panel members prior to completion of the process.

The thank-you letter aims to:

- influence the decision-making process through building on your relationship with the panel
- provide additional supporting information
- correct any wrong impressions you felt were made at the interview (but use a non-defensive tone)
- help you stand out more against the other applicants.

You may also use your gained knowledge of the hidden criteria (refer to Section 3) to build on your case for selection. Include mention of your ongoing and strong commitment to the job. Finally, you may be able to provide useful ideas on their business that could show the value added in employing you. Be careful that you do not criticise them or look too arrogant in this.

Clearly, if they make their final decision on the day, then there is nothing you can do about it, though there is no harm in sending the letter anyway. They may remember you for the next job opportunity!

Enclose any documents you promised to forward or maybe helpful websites that came up in your discussion. Be careful not to send original documents unless absolutely necessary as they may be lost. As an alternative, consider sending a certified copy of the originals. Certification may be made by a justice of the peace or a commissioner of declarations. You must have the original and the copy for them to certify, but at times, they prefer to make the copy themselves as it is easier to certify without closely checking a copy made by you. Search the Internet for local contact lists of such authorised persons. Remember to complete this follow-up strategy as quickly as possible to demonstrate how keen and organised you are.

Other Strategies

In addition to considering the thank-you letter, you may also call to reinforce how much you would like the job and ask whether there were any reservations about your interview that you could maybe clarify.

Do not harass the interviewer by persistent follow-up calls or further letters, or you may be seen as a nuisance and even have a favourable decision reversed! Continue to job-hunt while you are waiting for an answer.

Remind your referees that they may receive a call. This is particularly important if it is your current boss or supervisor of a current job. Remember that in some circumstances, the employer or agency may seek reports when deciding on the shortlist for interview. You may have received a job offer subject to good referee reports and a medical. Many jobs are now also requiring a criminal records check, Working with Children Check or police clearance. Provide one if it is requested prior to the interview, but be aware that they usually last only twelve months. An employer may still want a more recent one, so be prepared to purchase a new clearance.

Post-Interview Self-Examination

To increase your chances of being successful in interviews, it is necessary to critically self-appraise your performance. Learn from your shortcomings and then work to improve your performance. Remember that we all could do better in hindsight. Very few would think that they said everything they could in the time available and while under pressure.

An organised person may develop a checklist to record their self-assessment, and it may include the following questions:

- Were you on time?
- Did you handle the initial greetings well and remember their names?
- Were you able to control your nerves and speak clearly?
- Did you maintain appropriate body language?
- Did you answer the questions well?
- Did you have problems with any particular question or test?
- Were you able to emphasise your strengths and minimise any weaknesses?
- What seemed to interest the interviewer the most?
- Did you talk too much or too little based on time taken or non-verbal feedback cues?

- Did you handle the interview close well and have an appropriate question or two?
- What could you have done better? How?

Remember to reflect on any feedback they gave you at the close.

Second Interviews

Subsequent interviews are more likely in larger organisations and with positions that are considered more complex or hold higher-level responsibilities. There may be an escalation from an external agency to the local Human Resources and management staff and to perhaps more-senior staff when the position has significant impact or influence on the operation or profitability of the business. At times, Human Resources staff may conduct follow-up interviews to expertly negotiate and determine salary and conditions. At this point, you are in a better position to negotiate than if seen by Human Resources staff earlier in the process. Their role in an early stage is more focused on screening for suitable applicants to progress to the next stage.

If offered a second interview, firstly, congratulate yourself as this means a decision has not yet been made and that you are of sufficient interest to see again. Then reflect on all that happened in the first one. Were there areas that the panel did not ask about? It could also be that there were some concerns raised at the first interview and the interviewer wishes to explore them further. This is thus another chance to reassure them of your abilities.

Continue your homework and prepare for new or maybe more in-depth questions. In case you have new people interviewing you, do not show annoyance at going over old ground again. It may be an opportunity to meet other more-influential people in the business. This can also facilitate other future job possibilities through building favourable relations via effective networking. Try to wear different clothes in this round, and again, bring your documents.

Remember to sell yourself again at the close. We all leave an interview thinking that we could have said more about this or that. Reflect on the conversation with yourself after the first interview, and prepare accordingly.

At times, the second interview may be worksite-based when the first was at an offsite screening centre. If this involves travel which is paid by the employer, then be modest in your costs and keep records. On other occasions, the second interview can be less formal and may, in fact, be over a meal or drink. Do not become overly comfortable with this but abide by all the general advice contained in this book as if you were attending a formal interview.

What if You Are Not Offered the Job?

Firstly, continue to fight for the job by expressing again your enthusiasm and commitment to working there. Rejection does not necessarily mean you did poorly, but there may be some perceived negatives you need to identify. You may not have had the best experience, abilities, or knowledge for that particular job. However, it is also possible that you were simply outclassed by somebody with higher or more relevant experience or qualifications.

Therefore, you can meet all the requirements of a job but not be competitive. A superior interview performance can change that through impressing the interviewer that you are the best choice for the post. In that scenario, better-qualified applicants can be beaten! You must demonstrate your potential to be the better choice in the long run.

There may have been a preconceived choice of an applicant (e.g. a current employee who is on a temporary contract). In other cases, there may have been other forms of bias against you, perhaps on a discriminatory factor, or you may not fit the stereotyped image of who they usually employ in the job. The interviewer may think that you will not fit in with their current team or culture. Thus, the interview process alone is not always the best way to choose the right person, and thus from your point of view, justice will not always prevail!

Ask for a debriefing to learn how you went and to gain valuable insight into your performance so that you can develop strategies for next time. Don't be too pushy in what you say (e.g. 'Can you tell me why I didn't get the job?'). It may work better to say something like 'Can you give me some feedback on how I might better position myself or meet your expectations for your next job opportunity?' Make notes on what is said, and even though you may disagree with some comments, you must remember that these are clues on what to change next time. Don't argue when given feedback as you may want to maintain a good relationship and keep them talking at this point.

If you cannot get this direct feedback, then alternatively make a personal record of how it went from your perspective, what you could do better, what you may need to practise more, what questions you were asked, etc.

If you have reason to believe that you did very well at the interview, then consider asking the interviewer to keep your application on file for any future positions. It would pay to call or write from time to time to refresh the interviewer's memory of your availability and continued interest. Don't make contact too often as you risk becoming an irritant. Keep contacts brief and perhaps only once every two or three months, especially in industries that may have regular staff turnover.

There are times when the selected applicant actually doesn't last long in that job, and the employer may come back to their list to give it to the next in line. So don't give up hope or burn any bridges!

Do not be disheartened by perceived rejection, and use every such opportunity as learning experiences. Believe that a better job awaits you elsewhere.

As stated previously, even a great interview performance will not guarantee a job as other biases may exist with the interviewers. However, should lack of success be ongoing, then it may be time for a reality check. Ask yourself if you are indeed seeking the right job for yourself. Seek professional guidance from a career centre, advisor, or consultant.

Handling the Job Offer after the Interview

You Are Offered the Job—What Next?

Firstly, clarify all the details of the offer. Check on start date, induction programmes, uniforms, parking, work hours, location and where to report, travel time to work, any pre-reading, details on the actual job, and your supervisor.

If the offer occurs after you have left the interview and you need further time to choose, make it reasonable, or you will seem to lack commitment, and they may consider withdrawing the offer. They may also be under time pressure to fill the job ASAP, and any delay has ramifications on their job product.

Also consider negotiating any planned holiday time or other work conditions of value to you. In other words, delay the final salary-level discussion till all other details are identified that will impact your decision on taking the job.

This is now the appropriate time to discuss salary and other conditions of employment. Be aware of market conditions for if you undervalue yourself at this point, it will cost a lot in the long run, and you lose leverage to negotiate after prematurely accepting their offer. Refer back to the section on dealing with questions about pay on what else to consider at this point.

If it is short-term or seasonal employment, consider whether it serves towards your ultimate employment goals.

Ensure that the employer has included all the conditions negotiated and not omitted any points agreed at the interview. Once all is agreed, you will need to confirm your acceptance and availability to start on the proposed date. Note that public-sector selection processes also usually include an appeal period so that any breach of relevant standards can be assessed before a contract is actioned. If a breach of standards did occur, then the entire selection process may need to be repeated. Therefore, a verbal job offer may not be actioned.

Tip: only resign from your current job once the job offer is finalised and in writing.

Don't burn your bridges by bad-mouthing your current employer as something could still go wrong with the new job and you may want or need to continue or even return later! They may also know your new employer!

You Get the Offer but Remain Undecided

If the offer is made at the actual interview or afterwards and you are unsure, then play for time. You may be waiting on another offer, or maybe there are factors associated with this job that need to be considered perhaps with a spouse or partner. It is probably a good strategy when seeking a new job to seek multiple interviews in a short time so you can weigh up the benefits of one offer versus another without delaying too long.

When you receive an offer, you must look enthusiastic but play for time by asking if you can confirm your acceptance after a brief time. Try not to make it greater than forty-eight hours, or you run the risk that they will cancel the offer if you look uncommitted or the delay is not tolerable. Don't try the tactic of ignoring the employer's calls as that sends a very negative message and will annoy them. Consider carefully before you disclose that you may be waiting on another offer. They may feel they are being blackmailed through perceived leverage for a better deal or feel betrayed after convincing them of your desire to work for them.

If the indecision is about the conditions offered by one employer versus another, then this is a time of negotiation. Your research on the job market should have yielded what is possible and thus reasonable to ask. Once you are offered a job, you have some leverage, but don't overplay it or risk having an offer withdrawn!

This can be a difficult time for new graduates who await their first choice of employer or perhaps their first choice has come back with a temporary contract only. Should you take an offer of permanent work from another employer or take the temporary work with your first choice while hoping it will lead to permanency in the future? The answer will depend on your personal circumstances and risk-aversion tendencies. Refer to the next section if you choose to reject the offer.

You Did Get the Job but Decided to Reject

There may be occasions where you choose not to continue with taking up the job offer. This may be due to receiving or accepting another offer elsewhere or that you formed a negative opinion of the business and no longer desire to work for them. In any event, don't burn your bridges as you never know whether you will be in a position to approach that company again in the future.

In some industries, there may be cross-business discussions of candidates, sharing of results, gossip, etc. If you make a good impression, then this can work for you, but if you do the opposite, then word of your shortcomings may go before you and dampen your chances elsewhere. This may be true of businesses or professions in relatively small or closed communities.

Thank them for the offer and their confidence in your abilities, and then withdraw from the offer politely and professionally. And state your reasons. Do it in a timely manner by withdrawing as soon as you have made your decision. They will appreciate not having their time wasted any further. In some circumstances, there may be a revised offer if they really want you, and you should be prepared to accept if it now meets your bottom line or better!

You Are Offered an Alternative Job with the Same Employer

Listen to the offer, clarify any points about what the job entails, and then ask for time to consider your position. Try to discover their reasons for offering a different job. Consider if it is worth entering the business on this basis and maybe trying for the original job once you have shown your abilities.

Section 5

Practice Questions

Guide to Interview Practice Questions

Disclaimer

The question examples presented here are just a selection of possible questions designed to get you thinking. Thus, the questions do not represent all possible questions to practise for an interview. Different jobs, occupations, and seniority will require different levels of sophistication. Additionally, there will be different levels of interviewer skills encountered. Although there is a substantial set of over 900 sample questions presented here, you may need to make modifications and adjustments to suit your industry. If there are other specific criteria (competencies) available for the job applied for, then be sure to consider possible questions for those criteria also. If you are unfamiliar with any terminology (e.g. lean thinking), then be sure to search the Internet for more information.

Format for Questions

Note: Words used in the following questions may be interchanged for others more suitable to the situation.

Examples:

- use of 'us' instead of 'me' where a panel is judging the interview
- use of 'school' instead of 'job' in the case of school-leavers without work experience
- use of 'staff' or 'subordinate' or 'peers' or 'customers' or 'clients'

- use of 'boss' or 'supervisor' or 'manager' or 'chief' or 'coordinator'
- use of 'task' or 'duty' or 'project'
- use of 'client' or 'customer' or 'patient' if a health-care worker
- use of 'business' or 'company' or 'organisation'.

A Note on Preparing Responses

It is best not to prepare answers in rote form as it may sound practised and may seem less genuine. It should be in your own language, using words you are comfortable and familiar with. Therefore, consider memorising the key points to the answer but make it mainly in your own words. You may be allowed to take some notes or index cards with your key points into the interview, but as stated elsewhere in this book, keep them clear and concise. Remember to practise the common, more-general questions and answers found in previous chapters.

Questions seeking examples should have, wherever possible, recent examples and also contain some complexity and variation between questions. It is not going to win you any points if you keep using the same example or one that is too simple. You want to demonstrate a depth in the use of your skills and experience. On the other hand, don't give too many examples and use up your valuable interview time or bore and irritate the interviewer. You can always check with them if they want to hear more.

Questions seeking accomplishments may prove hard to answer while under pressure, and thus it is recommended that this be an important part of your preparation. Try to list all positive examples ranging from small feedback incidents to any major recognition awards. The latter are not always part of job cultures, and so the seemingly ordinary examples may suffice (e.g. a congratulatory email, a great performance appraisal, feedback from top staff on a project well done, or an incident well managed). The question sets that follow may also guide you in considering where you may have excelled.

Question Samples by Criteria, Competency, or Attribute

The following lists may prove useful when practising for an interview or as ideas for those conducting interviews. They are in alphabetical order by subject heading and based on job selection criteria and other attributes relevant to job requirements. Complex scenario questions are not included as they must be appropriate to the real job, though using these sample questions will still help in preparing responses.

Adaptability

(Refer also to the problem-solving section.)

What kinds of problems did you run into when moving from one department/job/school to another? How did you overcome them?
Do you have any examples of when the usual methods to do something failed suddenly and you had to do the task in a new way?
Do you have any examples of when the tool you needed for the job was missing and how you still completed the job?
Which supervisor/boss has been the hardest to work for, and why?
There have been a number of workplace reforms. How have you managed to cope with the changes?

Ambition

(Refer also to the section under motivation.)

Where do you see your career going in, say, five years?
Do you have a five-year plan for your career?
What are your career goals?
Have you considered any other goals?
What have you done towards achieving your goals?
In what areas do you lack skills/knowledge/qualifications? How do you plan to meet these needs?
What are your ambitions with respect to work?
Have you done the best work you are capable of?
Where do you see yourself going in this business?

Analytical Ability (Financial)

Describe the kind of financial reports you have experience with. How are they used? How much analysis work have you done with them?
What was the most complex financial analysis you have done?
Describe how you may prepare a budget forecast.
Is your work used at a departmental or organisational level?
Do you get it right the first time?
What experience did you gain in school with accounting methods?
Discuss your experience in examining and interpreting financial trends.
What factors do you take into account when conducting a trend analysis?

Analytical Ability (General)

(Refer also to the sections on problem-solving, critical thinking, and investigative ability.)

What are examples demonstrating your good analytic ability?
How do you go about analysing problems and determining their solutions?
What process do you use to consider solutions to work problems?
If you are provided with a number of facts about a client, how do you go about identifying their needs? (This is especially applicable to health occupations.)

Approachability

What would colleagues say about your approachability, and why?
How do you remain approachable at work?
What makes you an approachable person?

Attention to Detail

(Note: The interviewer may ask questions in relation to a particular work function, process, task, report-writing, etc.)

Describe how you prevent errors in your work.
Describe how you ensure all the details are covered in your work.
Tell us about a time when your attention to detail was critical to success.
Tell me about a time when you found an error in your work. What did you do about it?
Has there been an occasion where you found a problem overlooked by others?

Describe a time when your attentiveness prevented a negative consequence for the department or business.
Describe a project where you had no margin of error.
Describe an occasion where something went wrong by slipping through the cracks.
Why is near enough not good enough in your work?

Autonomy

(Refer to the section on independence.)

Career Goals and Development

Where do you plan to be in five years (or ten years)?
What is your plan for your career?
What steps will you take to advance your career?
What steps have you taken in the past year to progress your career?
How have your previous jobs assisted towards meeting your career goals?
What further training have you undertaken to advance your career?
Have you sought feedback or guidance on your goals?
What career options do you have at present?
How do you progress and keep track of your goals?
Have you had to take a step backwards in order to advance your goal?
Can you give an example of when you had to make a difficult career choice?

Change Management

Give an example from your experience when you had to deal with a situation where old practices have been altered or replaced with new ones.
Describe the principles of change management.
Describe when you have introduced a substantial change at work.
Staff can be resistant to change, so how can you engage them to embrace the new change?
What is the secret to winning over staff when culture change is needed?
What is the role of change champions, and how do you choose them?
How do you firstly identify and then overcome barriers to change?

Coaching and Mentoring Others

Do you always use the same approach to coach others?
Are you aware of different ways (adult learning styles) to coach people?
What do you like most about coaching others?

Why might people need coaching?
How do you overcome any interpersonal problems when in a coaching role?
What is the difference between supervision and mentoring?
Describe how you have coached or mentored others in their work.

Commitment to Learning (Ongoing Education)

(Refer also to the section on professional commitment.)

What courses or educational events have you attended over the past year?
What courses or educational events do you plan to attend over the next year?
How do you keep informed about changes in your profession?
What work-related articles have you read recently?
What have you gained through attending the courses you have listed in your résumé?
Have you been able to apply at work the actions that you have learned in courses?
What are your career goals over the next five years?
What steps have you taken to improve your performance at work?

Communication Skills (General Skills)

(Refer also to the sections on written skills, presentation skills, and particular attributes—e.g. negotiation skills.)

How may you vary your communication style to suit different people you deal with?
Tell us about a time you worked with a person of a different culture and accent.
Tell us about your experience working in a culturally diverse workplace.
What type of communications do you prefer, and why?
Why do you believe you possess good communication skills?
What skills or abilities do you have that make you good at communication?
How do you recognise good communication skills in others?
Do you have any examples of when you improved communications within the workplace?
We all experience communication barriers at times. What strategies do you use to overcome such barriers?

Tell us about a situation where you failed to communicate appropriately. What could you have done differently?
What can you do to make your communication with others more effective?
How do you establish good communication and information flow with others?
What techniques can you use to help others understand your point?
Describe a time when your communication skills got you out of trouble.
Describe a time that you had to deliver bad news or a poor appraisal.
Tell me about a time when you had to give someone difficult feedback. How did you handle it?
How did you or would you handle a situation where somebody publically criticises you?
Can you be assertive when needed? Describe the situation.
How do you know when others have understood you?
How do you know if others are listening, and how do you show you are listening to them?
How do you use non-verbal cues to help communications?
Describe a situation in which you had to use good oral communication skills to convince others.
Tell us about a time that you had to carefully explain something to another employee or customer.
Describe a time when you had to explain something technically complex to a colleague. What problems did you come across, and how did you deal with them?
Describe your methods when needing to present complex information in a simplified manner to your listeners.
Describe why you believe you are effective at team or client presentations.

Community Involvement or Commitment

What do you enjoy doing on the weekends or for leisure time?
Are in involved in any recreational or community organisations? At what level of participation?

Confidentiality

In this department, confidentiality is necessary. Describe a similar working environment you have experienced.
What must you do to maintain confidentiality in your work?
Why is confidentiality important in our work?

What information is OK or not OK to give callers?
What are our legal obligations with respect to confidentiality?
Have you ever had to reveal a work secret, and why?
What are the consequences of breaking confidentiality?

Conflict-Resolution Skills
(Refer also to the negotiation and mediation sections.)

Tell us about a conflict situation you experienced and what you did about it.
How do you go about resolving conflict?
If a conflict is proving difficult to resolve, what other steps may you take?
How do you avoid conflicts in the workplace?
Why do conflicts occur in the first place?
Can you tell us about the win-win concept, and why aim for that outcome?

Coordination Ability
How do you achieve coordination of activities across your department?
How many work groups have you had to coordinate?
How do you manage to get groups to work together?
What is the relationship between your department and others that rely on your work?
Who or what do you usually have to check on before making a decision?
What skills do you have that make you a good coordinator?

Creativity
(Note: this may also be tested by brain teaser questions—e.g. 'Tell me ten other things I can do with this pen'.)

Do you often come up with new ideas at work? Outline.
Are you known for any innovations at work? Explain.
Have you encouraged any innovations at work? Outline.
Describe some new ideas or ways of doing things that you have created.
Tell us about a time in which you developed an unconventional approach to solve a problem.
What are some of the best ideas you have come up with at work?
In what ways are you creative?
What do you do differently than others in your job?

What kinds of problems have you solved at work? Explain.
What was the most imaginative way you had of selling an idea or product?

Critical Thinking

(Refer also to the sections on problem-solving and analytical ability.)

How do you go about problem-solving?
Tell us about the steps you took to develop a new project.
Tell us about how you identified things to improve and change at work.
Why would you say that you are a critical thinker?

Customer Service

How do you deal with difficult (angry) customers?
If a customer presents a complaint, describe the steps you would take.
What is meant by customer service?
What makes you good at customer service?
Have you initiated any improvements to customer service?
Tell us of a time when company policies seem to cause problems with good customer service and what actions you took.
What issues can there be between business interests and customer interests, and how do you manage any differences?
Describe the steps you take to achieve a high level of customer satisfaction.
What skills and attributes do you have in customer service?
How do you win over customers?
How do you identify customer expectations and meet them?
Have you turned down a request from a customer? Why? And explain how you managed the situation.
Tell us of a time when a customer was not satisfied with the service you provided.
Tell us of a time when your customer service skills were actually praised.
Have you ever taken initiatives to solve customer concerns that were considered above and beyond your duties?
When have you demonstrated customer service that was considered above normal expectations?
Tell us about situations in which you had to be very tactful when dealing with staff or the public.

Decision-Making

How do you go about making decisions?
What types of decisions did you make in your last job?
When do you need to consult others over a decision?
Can you give an example of when you had to be very decisive?
What kinds of decisions can you make quickly compared to slower ones?
Describe a problem situation in which you had to give a quick decision.
If you have to make an immediate decision, what factors do you consider?
Describe a situation where you had to change your decision after implementing your actions.
Can you give an example of when a decision took some time to make? Why was it difficult?
How long have you taken to make a decision?
What decisions do you find hardest to make? Why?
What are some of the biggest, most important decisions you have made in the past year?
Rarely are situations one dimensional. When did you have to handle a situation that had many factors to consider?
How have you gone about making business decisions?
How have you gone about making decisions that affected your career?
Describe a time when your decision was not the right one. What could you have done differently?
Describe a situation when you had to make an unpopular decision (or one that carried the risk of a negative impact on the business).
Describe a decision you made that was unpopular and how you handled implementing it.
Describe some work problems and how you went about fixing them.
Give an example of a situation where you had to make a decision when you didn't have all facts.
Give an example of competing deadlines and how you managed it.
Discuss why you delayed a decision in order to gather more information.

Delegation

When is it appropriate to delegate work/tasks?
What do you delegate to others?
How have you managed delegating work to a group?
What kinds of decisions can you delegate to others?
Give me an example of when you last delegated some work?

Do you find that when you delegate work, it is not done properly and it is better doing it yourself?
When did you last delegate work to discover it was not done properly or on time? Describe.
Do you believe doing it yourself is better, or are you happy with delegating work?
When have you taken back delegated work, and why?
How do you feel about delegating work?
What stops you from delegating more?
Have you done much overtime lately? Why was it necessary?
Explain your biggest mistake in not delegating?
Explain your biggest success in delegating?
Do you get others to help you when your workload is getting too busy?
How much direction do you need to give when delegating work?
How much monitoring or follow-up is required when you delegate?

Education

(Note: you can replace the word 'school' with 'college', 'university', or other training institution as relevant.)

What school did you attend? What did you think of it? Why?
What did you like most/least about your school? Why?
What subjects (courses) did you do?
Which subjects did you like most? Why?
Which subjects did you like least? Why?
Why did you choose those subjects?
What do you attribute your success in school to?
What did you think of the teachers?
What do you think of your exam results?
What is your philosophy on education?
What are current issues in education?
Tell us what you know about the curriculum framework and how you use it in daily teaching.
How do you stay up to date professionally?
How have you maintained and updated your knowledge since leaving school?
What new skills have you picked up in the past twelve months?
How will what you have learned help you in this job?

What training course(s) have you attended, and how did they prove useful to your work?

Energy and Enthusiasm

When in the day do you get your best work done? Why?
When in the day do you tackle your toughest assignments? Why?
How do you get through your workday?
Do you find work tiring or exhausting? Explain.
What do you find most tiring about your work?
What do you consider good reasons to postpone tasks/assignments?
How do you manage your time to achieve all your duties?
Do you often need to work overtime?
How much physical energy does your day need? How do you cope?
What are the longest hours you have worked? Why?
What is the highest number of consecutive shifts you have worked?
How have you found working shift work?

Environmental Awareness (Extra-organisational)

How do you keep informed of what is happening in the sector/industry?
What government agencies affect your operations?
How do you keep up to date with what is happening?
What magazines or reports do you read each month?
What factors outside this organisation affect your work?
What events in the foreseeable future may impact on this business? How?

Experience (General)

(Note: if you have already left your past job, the tense of the following questions would change to 'Why did you . . . ?' This is an area for good preparation prior to the interview. Be clear about your past work and be prepared to succinctly recount this history, focusing on aspects most relevant to the job applied for! Prepare your thoughts on any special challenges and good results—achievements, targets, KPIs, etc.)

Tell us about your work history.
Tell us about your current job. What exactly do you do?
What are your major duties or responsibilities (or major projects completed)?
How does this job differ from your current job?
What do you like about your current job?

What do you dislike about your current job? Why do you want to leave?
In your job, what do you find most difficult to do?
How would you rank your performance against others in the same role?
What do you think of your colleagues? What do they think about you?
What do you know of our company?
What do you know about our products/services?
Have your responsibilities changed recently? Please explain.
Do any of your duties cause you frustration? If so, which ones?
Why are you planning to leave?
Describe your work at [enter company name where employed previously].
Describe your experience in [enter process name here].
What experience have you had in/at [enter process here]?
What is your greatest achievement?
Why should we employ you?
What can you offer us?
What value will you add to our business?

Experience (Machines)

What equipment did you operate at [enter company name where employed previously]?
What tickets (certifications) do you have?
What experience do you have in operating [enter equipment name here]?
What is your error rate?
What is your speed rating?
What is your safety record?
Tell us about the equipment you are proficient with.
Outline the equipment/machinery you have used and your proficiency level with each one.
When did you last use [enter equipment name here]? And what for?
Explain how to operate [enter equipment name here] safely.
What maintenance is required on [enter equipment name here]?
Outline the maintenance programme for [enter equipment name here].

Experience (Process Operation)

Describe the steps involved in [enter process here]?
Have you learned any shortcuts?
How do you observe safety protocols when using [enter equipment name here]?

Experience (Proficiency)

How successful are you at your work? How do you know?
Have you won some form of recognition for your work?
How does your work compare to your colleagues'? How do you know?
How do you rate your proficiency on [enter item name here]? Why?

Family

(Note: Many, if not all, family-oriented questions will be irrelevant to the job and, in fact, may contravene discrimination legislation.)

What does your family think about your application for this job?
What is the value of family versus work commitments?
What do your parents do?

Flexibility

In what ways do you believe you act with flexibility at work?
Describe a project where you had to overcome an obstacle. How did you get around it?
Describe a situation where you had to change your approach in order to succeed.
Changes often occur in workplace processes. Describe how you have managed a change in how things are to be done.
How do you overcome barriers in your work?
Describe a situation where you believe you have shown great flexibility in your work.
Describe a situation where you had to alter the usual processes to get the job done.
How do you feel about changes in the workplace, such as new policy or procedures?
How do you feel when during a workday, your supervisor gives you new priorities when you had already planned your day and priorities?
Give some examples of when you had to approach several team members individually about a project or problem and how you may have had to alter your approach.
What do you do if you don't initially win support for an idea?
What do you do if a new project has been given to you without any guidelines on how to achieve it?

Some jobs have work rotations in different areas and often with different work cultures. How do you cope with that?

Goal Orientation

How do you develop personal and professional goals?
How do you ensure you meet them?
When have you had to change your goals, and why?
Have you ever accomplished something you didn't think you could?
Can you provide examples that show you are goal-oriented?
Give an example of a goal you reached, and tell me how you achieved it.

Honesty

(Refer also to the section on integrity.)

Have you found it necessary to bend the truth in your job? Explain how this happened. (NB: may be necessary to maintain government secrets.)
Staff are known to take little items home, such as pens and scissors. What do you think of this? (NB: a trap question!)
How have you demonstrated honesty at work?
How do you instil honesty in your employees?

Independence

Have you worked without much guidance? Please explain.
Do you like working with others or alone?
In your past employment, have you ever had to work without close supervision? How did you manage that?
Describe a situation in which you had to work independently. Were you commended on your actions?
Describe a situation not covered by company policy that you had to manage.
Has there been an occasion where you had to work around company policy, and why?
What kinds of independent decisions do you make in your current/past job?
How often do you have to ask for advice before commencing a new task/ solving a problem?
Under what circumstances do you think you must consult with your supervisor/boss before taking action?
How often do you meet up with your boss, and why?
What do you do in your job that may not be covered by your job description?

What constraints in decision-making do you have to work under?
Describe a situation that you had to manage on your own.
How do you know when you are doing a good job?

Information Technology (IT) Skills

Describe which software programs you use and their versions (relevance), when last used (currency) or how often (frequency), and your competence level (beginner to expert user).
What initiative do you need at work? Do you design reporting functions or just use them? Also, outline the complexity of reports generated.
What programming language abilities do you have, and what have you done with that knowledge (i.e. create/develop to repair other people's work)?
What help roles have you been responsible for, and what complex problems have you solved?
What is your opinion on *x* program, and do you believe better ones exist?

Initiative

(Note: Knowledge and investigation of the current job and company/business background are always a good sign and may be tested. Reading department policies, vision statements, mission statements, value statements, etc. or meeting key people before the interview may also demonstrate initiative.)

Explain any situations where you have had to use your initiative to get the job done.
Have you been recognised for your initiative by your past supervisor or employer? Please explain.
Do you present your views and opinions on work practices? Please give an example.
When starting a new project, how much help do you need?
Tell us of a time that you were unable to complete the delegated task for whatever reason, and what did you do?
What do you do differently than other staff? Why?
Have you found ways to make your job easier, more interesting, or more successful?
Have you found ways to make your subordinates' jobs easier/more interesting/more successful?
Have you improved workflow in some way that others had not thought of?
What ways have you changed your current job?

We all face obstacles or barriers in our work. Tell us about such a situation that you prevented from eventuating through good planning.
Tell me about some ideas or suggestions you have put forward to your current/previous employer/supervisor? Were they accepted? If not, why not?
Have you ever done more than what is required of your job? In what way? Why?
Tell us about a time you were rewarded or recognised by management for your efforts.
Tell us about a time you used higher than average initiative at work.
Tell us about a time in which you had to take control and act without instructions from above.

Integrity

(Refer also to the sections on confidentiality and honesty.)

Have you ever been caught breaking a company rule or policy? How close did you come?
Have you ever had to bend or break the rules to get the job done? How?
Everybody has to bend or break the rules sometimes. Can you give an example of when you have had to do this?
Have you found it necessary to bend the truth in your job? Explain how this happened.
How did you handle a request to do something that is outside your morals or ethics?

Interpersonal Skills (General Questions)

(Refer also to sections on particular attributes—e.g. flexibility.)

Do you find yourself able to get along well with people? Explain.
What are the steps that you take to maintain good co-worker relationships?
How do you initiate relationships with other co-workers?
What problems do you have getting along with others?
How would you feel about working for someone who knows less than you?
When have you had difficulty getting along with another person, and why? What did you do?
How frequently do you support others and receive support from others?
What irritates you about other people, and how do you deal with it?

Give an example of how you have handled difficult members of the public in your last job.
Describe a situation at work that made you angry. What was the result?
Describe a time when you had to change other people's negative attitude. What did you learn from this experience?
What is the value of networking, and how do you go about developing networks?

Investigative Ability

(Refer also to sections such as problem-solving and analytical ability (general).)

Describe a project that required gathering a lot of information and how you went about it.
Have you had to gather data from a number of sources in order to make a decision? Describe.
Describe your last major report and how you went about researching your information.
If you had to do this project (example provided), where would you begin?

Lateral Thinking

(Refer also to the creativity and initiative sections.)

What techniques can be used at work to encourage lateral thinking?
What conditions do you need at work to foster lateral thinking?
What can you tell me about the *Six Thinking Hats* by Edward de Bono?
Can you give examples reflecting your ability to think laterally?
When have you had to think laterally at work?
Do you know any lateral thinking techniques? Explain.

Leadership

(Refer also to the sections on management and people management.)

Do you consider yourself a leader (or natural leader) at work? Why?
What sort of leader would your team describe you as?
Do you think a leader should be feared or liked?
Do you have any examples of when you displayed leadership (or took on a leadership role) at work/school?

What skills do you believe good leaders need to have?
What are the key values of a leader? How do you demonstrate these values?
Tell us what you think leadership entails.
Have you had to win cooperation from a group over an unpopular decision (or a new way of doing things)? How did you do it?
Have you had to convince a team to work on a project they weren't happy about? How did you do it?
Do you need power or authority as a leader?
Have you been in a position of authority in a previous work? How did you exercise that authority?
How often do you need to meet with your team? Why?
How do you run your meetings?
What role do you usually play at meetings (especially with peers, interdisciplinary groups, management committees, etc.)?
How do you resolve problems with staff?
Do you have any staff members who do not work well together? What have you done to improve this situation?
When leading a working party or committee, did you manage to get what you wanted from the group?
Describe a time when you were in the lead role for a project.
What is your leadership style?
Do you vary your leadership style? How, when, and with whom?
What is the difference between a manager and a leader?
When do you involve staff in decision-making?
When do you make decisions by yourself?
Give an example of a recent decision that involved input from your staff?
Do you set goals or objectives for yourself/department? How did you go about setting them?
Have you had any problems getting staff to accept your goals/objectives?
Describe a situation where your leadership was considered at fault.
Have you had to reprimand staff, and if so, how?
How do you win staff over to your point of view?
How can you get a group to vote your way?
How do you get staff to work towards a common goal?
How do you keep each member of the team involved and motivated?
How do you help staff with performance problems?
How do you set a good example for your staff?

Leisure Interests

How do you relax?
What interests do you have?
Do you have any hobbies?
Do you like sports?
Do you belong to any teams?
Do you belong to any clubs?
Do you read much?
What do you like to watch on TV?
What sort of books have you read?
Which newspaper or articles (including web-based ones) do you read?
How much time do your leisure activities take up?
Do you play any leadership role in your leisure activities?

Listening Skills

Do you have good listening skills? If yes, how do you know?
Please explain why you believe you have good listening skills.
What attributes does a good listener have?
Why is it important to listen attentively?
Can you give an example of when you had to follow detailed verbal instructions to complete the job? How did it go?
What could be the consequences of poor skills in this area?
How do you show others that you are listening to them?
Can you give an example of when you may have misinterpreted instructions given to you? Why do you think it happened?

Management Skills (General)

(Refer also to the sections on leadership and people management.)

How would you describe your management style?
How do you like to be managed?
How do you manage people?
What do you dislike as a manager?
Are there certain types of people you don't like to work with?
Have you ever had to fire a person (or come close), and why?
What is the most difficult task to do as a manager?
What was your toughest decision to make as a manager?
When have you had to handle a situation out of the ordinary?

What have you been criticised about in the past?
What makes you a good manager?
What are your strengths as a manager?
Why do you think you have management potential?
What skills and attributes do you own as a manager?
What are factors you would associate with good management?
How do you manage difficult employees, such as ones who will not do more than the basic duties outlined?
Do you prefer hands-on or delegation? Why?

Mediation Skills

(Refer also to the negotiation section.)

Can you provide an example of when you have had to act as a mediator in the workplace?
What are important principles in mediation?
As a mediator, what process would you follow?
What skills and attributes do you have that make you a good mediator?
How do you avoid taking sides when mediating between two parties/people?
Describe a difficult mediation exercise. Explain why it was and your actions.

Mentoring

(Refer to the coaching section.)

Motivation (Self)

What do you enjoy about your current (or past) job(s)?
Provide some examples of what you found most satisfying in your last job.
What has been the highlight of your career?
Who would you say has had the most influence on your life, and why?
What are examples of decisions you have made that had a significant impact on your career?
What gave you the greatest sense of achievement in your past work?
What did you dislike or was least satisfying about your current (or last) job?
Can you give any examples of when your work became too routine or mundane and what you did, if anything?
Why do you want to leave your current job?
What aspects of your past work did you find frustrating?

Can you provide any examples of work improvements you initiated?
Can you give an example that indicates your willingness to work hard?
Why are you interested in this line of work or in working here?
What do you look for in a job?
What are your long-term goals?
What are some recent responsibilities you have taken on, and why?
Provide examples that illustrate your ability to be self-driven in your work.
Would you say you are self-driven? Provide examples to support that.
How do you measure your success at work?
Tell us about an example of when you set and achieved your goal(s).
Where do you see yourself with respect to your work/career in five years?
Is salary or job satisfaction more important to you?
What do you think is needed to be successful in the job?
What subjects did you enjoy most at school and why?
Which job did you like best, and why?
What motivates you to produce your best at work?
What did your boss do to get the best out of you?

Motivation (Others)

How do you get the best out of your staff?
In what ways do you motivate staff to achieve higher productivity?
Provide an example of how you were able to motivate employees or co-workers.
Staff can react poorly to change, so how do you go about managing change so that staff performance doesn't slip?
Some staff members can be described as having plateaued in their career and show no enthusiasm at work. How would you deal with that?
Do you have good motivational skills? Explain.
How do you discipline staff without also destroying any motivation they have?
What tools or actions do you take to motivate staff?
What do you think drives staff to do better at work?
How do you get staff to work towards a common goal?
What factors can either demotivate or motivate staff to perform at work?
If you experienced low employee productivity, what did you do about it?
If your section/department is considered below benchmark, what would your actions be?
Discuss how you engage other staff in training or coaching.

Negotiation Skills

(Refer also to the mediation section.)

What skills do you need to be a good negotiator?
Tell me about a tough negotiation experience.
How do you prepare for an encounter that will require negotiation?
Give us an example of a great idea you had to negotiate an agreement on.
Give us an example of a great idea you failed to negotiate an agreement on.
Tell me about the win-win concept in negotiation.

Occupational Health and Safety

What do you know of the occupational health and safety legislation?
How do you maintain a safe working environment?
What do you understand by the term 'duty of care'?
As a supervisor, how do ensure the safety of your staff?
As an employee, what are your responsibilities with respect to safe work practice?
How would you set up a safety programme at work?
What safety requirements are applicable to your work?
Has any of your staff been injured on the job? What happened?
We all have to bend the safety rules sometimes. Can you give an example of when you had to do this? (NB: may be a trap question!)
Have you had to discipline an employee for breaking safety rules? Explain the situation.
Give an example when you witnessed staff breaching the hygiene/sanitation rules. What did you do about it?
Discuss what sanitation (hygiene) rules (or health standards) apply in this job.
Have you conducted or instigated any safety audits? What factors were checked?
Have you been involved in any investigations on accidents? Describe the process.

Organisational Ability

(Refer also to the sections on time management and planning.)

Have you organised any events? How did they go?
How do you remain organised?

How do you efficiently manage a heavy workload?
What is the most difficult/complex event you have organised?
How do you cope with an unexpected interruption to your work schedule?
How often do you suffer interruptions? Is there anything you can do to reduce them?
Describe a reorganisation at your work and your part in it.
How do you keep track of things that need your attention?
How do you keep track of jobs you have delegated?
How do you prioritise the day-to-day tasks?
How would you go about organising [enter task here]?
What are some recurring problems in your area? What have you done about them?
How do you run your staff meetings? How do you organise actions?
Give us an example of an important goal you set yourself and tell us how you went about reaching it.

People Management Skills

(Refer also to the sections on management, leadership, teamwork.)

What do you do that may irritate others?
What do people like about you?
Why would you say you have good people skills?
What problems do you have getting along with others?
What attributes do you have that make you a good people person?
How do you know if you are being an effective manager?
In what ways do you vary your approach to people of different backgrounds or cultures?
How do you change if feeling stressed or under pressure?
How do you react to other people's mistakes?
Describe a time when your team did not meet your expectations. Why?
How did you deal with an angry customer?
Tell us about a time you worked with a person that became easily offended or defensive.
How do you build staff loyalty to you?
How do you motivate (inspire) staff to work at their best?
When have you inspired people at work?
What can cause staff to lose motivation in their work?
What do you think staff want (expect) in their job?

What could you improve in your people management skills?
How do you manage poor-performing staff?
What would you do if a staff member is displaying poor teamwork?
What has been your experience in dealing with the poor performance of a subordinate, and how did you go about it?
How do you deal with difficult staff?
How do you go about disciplining your staff?
How do you go about rewarding your staff?
Discuss how you adapt your management style when dealing with a variety of different people.

Persuasiveness Ability

How do you go about winning people over to your point of view?
How successful are you in winning people over to your side?
How do you go about selling an item to a disinterested customer?
How do you get a customer to buy something different (and more expensive!) than they set out to buy or if their first choice was unavailable?
Give some examples of great ideas you have persuaded your colleagues or boss to adopt.
Give me some examples of any of your great ideas that were not adopted.
Describe a time when your great idea was not adopted.
Describe your most satisfying experience in getting your idea accepted by management?
Describe your most disappointing experience in getting your idea accepted by management?

Planning Skills

(Refer also to the sections on time management and organisation.)

What kind of planning activities have you been involved in?
Describe a typical day/week.
How do you prioritise tasks in your workday?
How did you plan last week's activities, and how did it turn out?
Do you have any short-term or long-term plans for your work unit?
What were your objectives over the past six months (past year), and how did you meet them?
What are your objectives this year? How do you plan on achieving them?
How do you keep track on the progress of your objectives?

How did you go about planning a typical project?
How many projects can you manage at the same time?
How did you prepare for this interview?

Policy-Writing

This position involves writing policy. Describe your experience in writing policies and how you go about it.
Explain the steps you take to develop new policy.
Outline the requirements of a good policy document.
Whom do you involve when writing or developing new policies?
How do you sell any new policies to employees?

Practical Learning Ability

Do you find it easy to learn new tasks? Give an example.
Are you quick to learn new tasks? Give an example.
How long did it take you to learn [insert task here—e.g. drive a forklift, operate particular machinery]?
How did you learn the technical aspects of your work at your previous job?
How did you go about learning to run the [enter name of process or equipment]?
What formal training have you had in [enter name of process or equipment]?
How good were you at it?
What parts of your training took the most time?
What parts of your training were the hardest?
What has been the most difficult task you have had to learn?
What has been the easiest task you have had to learn?
What subjects in school gave you the most difficulty?

Presentation Skills

(Refer also to the sections on communication, written communication, and public speaking.)

How many presentations have you made to a group to date? How about in the past year?
Can you give examples of some of the presentations you have done?
How do think your last presentation went? Did you receive any feedback on your performance?
Would you have done anything better?

What audiovisual aids did you use (have you used)?
How do you (did you) keep the audience's attention?
How can you use your voice to stimulate your audience?
What skills do you use during presentations to engage the audience?
What skills do you consider important in an oral presentation?
What can you do to facilitate a more effective presentation?
How did you (would you) prepare for a presentation?
What has been the most demanding presentation you have done? Why was it?
What has been the most difficult presentation you have done? Why was it?
What has been the most important presentation you have done?
What questions were you asked in your last presentation? Were you able to answer them?
We all get questions we cannot answer from time to time, what do you do when this happens?
Are you nervous when presenting?
How do you handle nerves when doing a presentation?
How do you help the audience to relax in a presentation?
How can you facilitate participation or engagement from your audience?

Pressure (Working Under)

(Refer also to stress section. ***Tip: Focus on good planning to reduce pressure.***)

Describe when you have had to work under pressure and how you coped.
What strategies did you use to cope with pressure?
Can you work under pressure or tension? How?
How do you work under pressure?
How do you respond when placed under pressure at work?
What makes you crack when under pressure?
Tell us about when you experienced anger on the job.
Have you ever failed to meet an objective at work? How did you cope with that failure?

Prioritisation Skill

(Refer also to the time management section.)

How do you prioritise your day's work?
When do you do the most important things in your day?

Do you ever finish the day without accomplishing your major task but instead have done many small tasks?
How do you cope with an unexpected interruption to your work schedule?
What do you do when two or more people give you work that competes for your time?
How do you determine the importance of tasks in your day?
How do you consider urgency versus importance in planning your day's tasks?
Describe what you would do when you are required to complete multiple tasks by the end of the day and there was simply not enough time?

Problem Solving

(Refer also to the section on analytical ability (general).)

How do you go about solving problems?
What techniques or strategies do you use to solve problems?
What are the steps you take to anticipate risks and resolve issues?
What skills do you bring forth when solving problems?
What are some of the problems you encounter in your work? How do you deal with them?
Tell us of an occasion where you solved a problem that others could not?
Tell us about a difficult problem you had to deal with.
Describe a time when your problem-solving and analytical skills were really put to the test.
Give an example of an innovative solution you created to solve a problem.
Describe a time that a project suffered several challenges and how you managed them.
How have you managed more than one project at once?
Tell us about when you introduced a work improvement.
What have you learned from your mistakes?
What problems frustrate you the most? How do you usually deal with them?
What kind of problems do you deal with the best?
Have you ever had a problem you could not solve, and why? ***(Tip: offer one you have since learned from!)***

Professional or Technical Interest and Commitment

(Refer also to commitment to learning section.)

How do you keep up to date with developments in this profession/trade?
Why do you think it important to keep up to date?
What are some important changes or issues happening in the profession/trade currently? How do you feel about these directions/issues?
What job-related associations/organisations have you joined? How long? What is your level of participation (e.g. committee member)?
What job-related lectures/workshops/seminars/conferences have you attended recently (in the past year)? What did you gain from them?
Do you read any professional/trade magazines? What articles have you recently found of interest?
What are your career goals over the next five years? What actions do you need to take to reach these goals?
Do you believe you have demonstrated a commitment to continuing education?

Project Management Skills

Describe your experience in managing a project.
Describe the steps you have taken in project management.
Describe how you documented your last project.
How do you plan and adhere to project timelines?
Tell us of a time you worked on a project team and about your role.
What was the last project you led, and what was its outcome?
How do you coordinate the many tasks and people involved in a project?
How do you plan a timeline for steps in a project?
Do you use any project planning tools or software?

Public Speaking

(Refer also to the presentation skills section.)

Have you ever done any public speaking? What feedback did you get?
How do you go about engaging the audience?
Tell us about your experience in public speaking.
How do you rate yourself as a public speaker? Why?
What do you do to manage nerves when in public-speaking events?
How do you deal with difficult audience members?

Do you utilise any audiovisual aids? Explain how.

Quality Improvement

(Note: Terms such as 'QA' (quality assurance), 'TQM' (total quality management), 'QI' (quality improvement), 'CQI' (continuous quality improvement) and 'best practice' may be interchanged with 'quality improvement' if such terminology is used at the worksite you are interested in. They are different aspects of quality methodology. The job specifications or duty list may use the relevant terminology they are seeking.)

What do you understand by the phrase 'quality improvement'?
What do you understand by the phrase 'best practice'?
Describe some QI projects you have initiated/participated in.
What do you understand by the phrase 'quality circle' or 'closing the loop'?
What do you understand by the term 'lean thinking', and have you any experience in that methodology?
Why is quality important in your work?
How may poor-quality work adversely affect this company?
How do you measure quality in this area?
Name some ways to assess the quality of your work.
What QA or improvement projects are relevant to the area applied for?
What ideas do you have for quality improvement projects?
Have you any experience with QA or improvement projects? Describe.
How do you evaluate the quality of your work and ensure that your work is of a high quality?
Discuss your QI experience and any problems encountered.
How can you be assured that you are providing a quality service?
What activities or measures would you implement in the *x* department to increase the efficiency and effectiveness of the department?

Rapport-Building Ability

When you commence in a new job/work area, how do you go about meeting people?
How do you go about being accepted into a work team?
How do you build rapport with people in the workplace?
How important is it for you to build rapport/relationships with other staff, your supervisor, or your clients/customers?
How do you show consideration to others?

Do you find it easy building positive relationships? Explain.
How do you cope with winning over difficult people?
How do you know if rapport has been established with others?
How can you judge whether your subordinates have established good rapport?
What feedback have you received to judge you are good with people?

Research

Describe a typical research process with the steps involved to completion.
What steps can you take to avoid any bias in the research?
Give an example of a research project you initiated or participated in, and outline your role and tasks.
Discuss the different research methodologies you are familiar with.
What methods can you use to obtain a random sample?
What experience do you have with research statistical methods?
How do you go about considering inclusion and exclusion criteria?
How do you estimate sample size to achieve statistical significance?
What do you understand by being blinded in research?
Do you have research publications or any funded projects? Discuss.
Discuss the importance of consent in research and how you may construct a consent statement.
What research funding sources may be applicable to this work?
Have you written a successful research funding request? Discuss.

Resilience

Describe a time in which you received negative feedback. How did you manage this feedback? What was the result?
Can you describe an event at work when things went wrong and how you coped following the event?
How do you bounce back after an upset at work?

Responsibility

In what ways has your experience to date prepared you to take on more responsibility?
In what ways do you show that you are a responsible employee?
How have you shown that you are able to take on greater responsibility?
When do you take responsibility at work?
Are there times when you do not accept responsibility at work? Explain.

Explain what responsibilities you take seriously at work.
What does taking responsibility mean to you?

Risk-Taking

(Refer also to the decision making section.)

Describe some recent decisions that carried the risk of getting it wrong.
How often do you make decisions that carry some risk?
Are you willing to take calculated risks? Explain.
Describe some decisions you have had to make without all the relevant information being available.
How far out on a limb have you gone to make a point?
Have you had to make a decision that was not yours to make? Explain.
Would you like more authority to make decisions? What kind?
Are you quick at making decisions? Describe the circumstances.
Describe a situation where you had to bend the rules to get the job done.
What has been the riskiest decision you have made?
Your decision to change jobs took some time. Why not sooner?
Describe a time when you didn't act even though you had considered the pros and cons.

Sales Skills

Sell me this *x*. (NB: interviewer will choose an object in the office.)
Describe your approach to customers.
How do you approach a customer who appears uncertain?
How do you build rapport with the customer?
Describe how you deal with difficult customers.
What questions do you ask that have the most success in leading to a sale?
What tactics do you employ to win a sale?
What do you say is your reason for success in sales?
Give an example when you successfully started or created a new sales or marketing technique.
What applicable sales experience do you have?
What do you consider to be your best sale or sales record?
What skills do you have in sales?
How do you keep up with new trends in sales and marketing techniques?
What makes a good salesperson?
What motivates you about working in sales and marketing?

How do you close the sale?
Tell us about your conversion rate in sales.
What has been the toughest sale you have experienced?
What do you consider was your most difficult sale? Why?
What do you consider to be your biggest sale?
Have you won any recognition awards for your sale level?
If a previous buyer came in to complain, what would you do?
Explain your follow-up practices.
What sales techniques do you use to promote a product?
What are some of the psychology behind how or why customers choose a product?
How do you use psychology to make a sale?
How do you go about selling an item to a disinterested customer?
How do you get a customer to buy something different (and more expensive!) if their first choice is unavailable?

Scope of Interests

Are you aware of current changes/directions in this organisation or [insert field or department or profession or industry here instead]? Explain.
How do keep informed on what is happening in this area?
What sources have you read recently to keep informed on what is happening in this field, profession, or industry?
If you were offered a transfer to another department in the organisation, which one would it be, and why?
Tell us about your leisure activities or interests out of work hours.

Self-Appraisal or Reflection

What was there about this job/course that made it a bit difficult for you?
What was there about this hobby/activity/job that appealed to you?
How would you assess yourself as a manager/salesperson?
How do you assess the quality of your work?
How would you describe your most-recent job performance evaluation?
What traits or skills do you have that might have accounted for your success?
If I were to call up your former supervisor and ask them what kind of person you were, what do you suppose they would say?
What have you learned from past jobs?
What have you learned from your mistakes?

How have you benefited from your disappointments?
What are you most proud of as a past achievement?
How do you feel about your work progress to date?

Sensitivity

Describe some situations where you thought you could have acted differently with somebody at work.
Are you able to make unpopular decisions? What was the last one you made, and how did it make you feel?
We all know somebody we deal with at work who wastes our time. How do you deal with that?
Do staff members often bring you problems? How do you deal with them?
How have you shown consideration for others?
How do you know when somebody is getting upset or frustrated with you?
How do you know when you are pushing too hard?

Software

(Refer also to the IT section.)

Be prepared for questions about software versions, currency of use, frequency of use, applications, etc. (NB. If you have not used a particular software but something similar in function, then talk about how you are familiar with using such software and your ability to quickly learn their preferred programs.)

Staff Development Ability/Experience

How do you go about getting the best out of your staff?
How do you recognise/identify your staff training needs?
How many of your staff are ready for promotion if an opportunity arises?
What are some of the common weaknesses in your staff? How would you tackle these weaknesses?
Do you have a staff development plan/process?
What techniques do you use in staff development?
Are you aware of different adult learning styles? Explain what you have utilised.
Tell me about some of your staff and your goals for their development.
Tell me about your greatest success in developing a staff member.

Tell us about a staff member who just couldn't seem to develop. What did you try?

Standards (Meeting or Developing)

How do you know if you are doing a good job?
How do know if others are doing a good job?
What distinguishes average performance from good or excellent performance?
How do you measure your success at work?
How you define doing a good job?
What do you look for when evaluating the standards of your staff?
What standards do you work to?
What standards are applicable to this workplace?
How do you keep your knowledge of the standards up to date?
What have you done to meet these standards?
Have you ever been unhappy with your performance? What did you do about it?
How have you differed with your past supervisors when judging your performance?
Tell me about a time when you may not have lived up to the expectations of your boss. What did you do after learning this?
How often have you missed deadlines? Why?
Do you consider the expectations on you (your work) to be reasonable?
Are you happy with your current department's performance? What areas could it improve in?
Can you give examples of when you may have worked above the standard required?
Can you give examples of when you considered your work to be below standard? Have you addressed this now?
Have you ever had to dismiss an employee? What were the circumstances?
Have you had to write any standards for your workplace? Explain how you went about it.

Strategic Planning

Tell us about a strategic planning process you have completed.
What steps do you take when preparing a strategic plan?
Give an example of a SWOT (strengths, weaknesses, opportunities, and threats) analysis.

Tell us about how your strategic planning skills have proven useful?
What do you research when undertaking a strategic planning process?
Whom do you involve when preparing a strategic plan?
What has been the outcome of previous strategic planning exercises?
Have you had cause to criticise a plan? Why, and what was the outcome?
What benefits were realised by the organisation in your last planning exercise?
How have you involved all stakeholders in a planning exercise?
Do you stick to your planned goals, or if you deviate, then why?
Have you assisted in the development of mission, vision, values statements as part of the planning process? Describe what you learned.
What differences might there be between short-term (two to three years) and long-term (ten years plus) plans?

Stress and Controlling Frustration

(Refer also to the section on pressure. ***Tip: as with questions on weaknesses, try to give an example and an action used to manage your stress, which means it can be controlled.***)

We all experience stress at times in our lives. In what ways have you experienced stress at work? How did you cope with it?
How do you manage stress in your work?
What stresses you in your work?
What kinds of pressure do you experience at work?
What situations give you the most pressure at work?
How often do you find it necessary to take work home?
When did you last lose your temper at work? What was the result?
What was your reaction the last time somebody lost their temper with you?
What frustrates you at work? What do you do about it?
Have you felt frustrated with others at work? How did you react?
Tell us about some times when you may have become frustrated or impatient with others at work (including customers). What did you do?
Have you been upset with yourself? Please explain.
How do you react when others do not agree with your suggestions?
Describe a time when you have been upset with another person at work?
Describe a time when you have been upset with yourself at work?
What personal sacrifices have you made in your job (for your boss)?

Supervision Ability (or Ability to Be Supervised)

(Tip: be personally open to direction and supervision, and recognise why it is sometimes necessary.)

Outline your experience in supervising staff (or students or apprentices).
Can you give an example of your ability to supervise or manage others?
What supervision responsibilities have you had?
What do you enjoy (or dislike) about supervising others?
What are some things your former supervisor did that you disliked?
Have you ever had to supervise former peers? How did you manage?
How do you feel about supervising staff who may be older and perhaps more experienced than you?
What supervision style works best for you?
How do you feel about taking direction?
Has your work or an idea that you proposed ever been criticised? How did it feel?
What kind of supervisor would you like to manage you?
What did you dislike about a former supervisor?
What are examples of things that you and your former supervisor disagreed about?
Do you ever have to change your supervision style with different staff? Explain.
Describe how you would supervise a new employee?
Describe the preferred relationship between a supervisor and those they supervise.
Describe how your approach to supervision may differ between a new employee and an experienced one in the area.
How do you assess the ability of your staff?
What procedures do you use to assess your subordinates' work?
How do you assess your own success at supervising staff?
How do you manage a staff member who is performing their work poorly?
What may be some reasons for poor performance? What actions would you take? What if they still don't improve?
Have you ever had to discipline one of your staff? Why and how?
How do you deal with a subordinate or student who disagrees with their appraisal?
How do you get the best out of your staff?

How do you keep track of what staff members are doing?
Describe the best and the worst boss you have worked for. Explain why you thought that.

Teamwork

(Tip: also consider non-work examples of great teamwork.)

What makes you a good team player?
What makes a good team?
Do you work well with others?
What kind of people do you find most difficult to work with? Why?
How does teamwork lead to better outcomes?
What are the pros and cons of working in a team?
What would be your ideal team to work with?
Do you prefer to work independently or with others? Why?
How well do you take direction?
How do create a good team?
How do you resolve conflict in your team?
How do you build the morale and effectiveness of a team?
How would you, as a team leader, recognise and regard the efforts of the members of your team?
How do you make each team member feel important?
What stages do teams go through from creation to maturity?
What do you do with a team member who appears destructive to the team?
What do you do when a team member is not pulling their weight?
What experience do you have working in a team?
How did you get along with the last team? Why did you think that?

Technical Ability

Tell me how you operate [enter equipment item here]?
What steps do you use in [enter job task here]?
What do you do for [enter condition here]?
How successful were you in [enter activity here]?
What legal issues will you need to be aware of in this role?
What standards are applicable to this job?
What safety issues are important to consider in this area?

Tenacity

Describe a situation where persistence has paid off.
Do you often see tasks through to their end?
How do you make sure tasks/projects are carried through to completion?
Can you tell of a project that only reached completion because of your persistence?
Describe a project that best demonstrates your tenacity.
What are some of the significant obstacles you have had to overcome to get where you are today?
Have you ever suggested a good idea that was not accepted? What did you do?
How long does it take you to complete an average assignment?
How many attempts would you make before giving up on a difficult task?
Why did it take you so long to complete your qualification?

Time Management

(Refer also to sections on prioritisation and organisation.)

How do you manage your time each day?
How do you plan your daily activities?
Do you often work back late? Why?
How do you keep track of things that are important (requiring your attention)?
How do you keep track of appointments?
How do you determine your top priorities?
How do you deal with interruptions?
When do you usually deal with paperwork?
When do you usually deal with follow-up phone calls?
What do you do when staff members are off sick or your workload is too much to handle in the day?
What do you do when the unexpected occurs and means that not all your work planned for the day is possible?
Do you have backlogs at work?
How do you catch up on possible backlogs of work after a vacation?
Do you generally meet your production targets/goal deadlines?
Give some examples of projects that you postponed. Why were they postponed?

Tell me about a time when you didn't meet a deadline.
Have you had to work overtime to complete your day's work? How much in the past few weeks?

Vigilance

How quickly does it take you to pick up that things are going wrong in your work or the work of others?
How do you monitor the quality of your work or that of others?
When working in unsafe areas/tasks, how do you make sure you or others remain safe?
Have you discovered some task or process being done unsafely? How did this come to your attention?
Have you discovered some task or process being done in a substandard manner? How did this come to your attention?
How do you remain aware of what is happening in your work environment?

Weaknesses

(Refer to the section on common interview questions, number 30.)

Tell us about a weakness (or the greatest weakness) of yours?
In what areas are you weak at work?
What weaknesses do you have, and what have you done about them?
What are you least confident about in your duties?
In what areas do you need to improve at work?
If anything in this job causes you to struggle, what would it be?

Willingness

You may be asked about your willingness to do something specific. ***(Tip: even if it appears menial at this point, it is better to agree as it may be a test of your ability to fit in with a team, and be prepared to do whatever it takes!)***

You may be asked about your willingness to work with certain types of people or demographics. It may also relate to their political or moral positions. ***(Tip: be wary of displaying discriminatory behaviours.)***

Working with Others

(Refer to the sections on teamwork and interpersonal skills.)

Written Communication Skills

(Refer also to the communication skills section. Note: Health professionals may get a question on knowledge of medicolegal aspects of written documents or within health records. Legal professionals may have questions around legal aspects of the printed word, phraseology, special formatting, etc. Secretarial or administrative staff may get questions on correct formatting of different types of documentation.)

What writing skills do you have?
What types of writing have you done? Give examples.
Who reads your work?
Can you provide an example of any reports you have written? Describe how you organised the content.
Give us an example of when you wrote a particularly good report.
Do you have any rules that you follow when writing reports? Explain.
Can you provide an example of any major projects you have written up?
What are (was) the most difficult writing tasks you have been given (or attempted)?
What has been your most important written work to date?
What has been the toughest writing assignment you have had to date? Why was it tough?
What reaction did you get to your work?
How difficult was it to do?
How did you approach the project/task?
What are you currently working on?
Do you have experience writing guidelines or instructions for others to follow? Did they work out the first time or require modifications? Explain.
How hard were they to write?
Are you experienced in writing policies? Can you describe one?
How important is formatting in a document?
What document formats have you any experience in?
Have you had to explain technical matters to people without a technical background? How did you manage?

Index

C

D

E

J

K

L

M

N

O

P

Q

R

S